Notes from the Margins:

Healing Conversations with God

Alane Pearce

Alane Pearce
P.O. Box 76381
Colorado Springs, CO 80907

ISBN- 978-0-9840753-0-0 printed;
ISBN- 978-1442169494 on Amazon.com

Cover design by John Wollinka, Design Corps
john@designcorps.com

Interior design by Alane Pearce Professional Writing Services
alane@Alane PearcePWS.com

Publishing and Marketing Support Provided by:
Jeff Pederson of JPED Consulting JPED56@comcast.net
Jay Heinlein of Heinlein Publishing Services
jay@heinleinpubservices.com

Notes from the Margins is dedicated to the praise and glory of Him who brought me out of the darkness and into the glorious light of the Lord. Not by might, not by power but by the moving of His Spirit.

Here's what people are saying about
                Notes from the Margins:

"Your book has been an inspiration to me. I've read it a few pages at a time to let the message soak in. The scriptures--so many of them that mean so much to you--are the ones I have leaned on during this long running family crisis that we are going through."

~Martha B.

"Thank you so much for putting your incredible story on paper for all to read. We have all gone through our own troubles but for you to come through yours and find God again is truly amazing. I walked away from God and my family when I was 15; I found him again--truly found him in April of 2009. He has sent me many miracles since then; your wonderful book was one of them."

~Kathie W.

Notes from the Margins is hands-down one of the most moving, powerful and personal accounts of pain and healing I have ever read. Alane takes her readers on a journey through loss, grief, and ultimately, the spiritual wholeness that can only come through God and His Word. A life-changing, life-giving book."

~Jocelyn Green
Faith Deployed: Daily Encouragement
for Military Wives

"A friend sent me your book and I just wanted to let you know that it was a comfort to me during a difficult part of my journey. I found it in my mailbox postmarked with the date that I was due with my fifth baby. You signed the book with a prayer for God to continue speaking healing and peace into my life; Notes from the Margins is the answer to that prayer.

I suffered three devastating losses; our pregnancies would be going along fine and then the baby would just die. I felt alone. I felt like God abandoned me. Eventually I felt nothing--it was better that feeling the pain. Then I read your book. I was reminded that God is here with us in our darkest hour. Thank you for sharing from the depths of your soul. Thank you for your honesty and your courage to write God's words. Thank you for helping me heal and to once again feel God's love."

~Michele F.

"I just wanted to tell you how much I enjoyed your book. I have never been so touched...It is clear to me that God is using you for his glory. I am giving this book to so many friends as I know it will help them through their trials in life. Thank you for sharing your faith."

~Linda O.

I am reading your book and feel like I am getting to know you better even though we have not met yet. Your strength is inspirational and your writing is great! I feel like we are having a conversation through the pages. You deserve a Delicious Life!

~Cynthia Nimerichter
DeliciousTheory.com

Shout Out:

Brandon--your support and encouragement through this process gave me the courage to continue. You are a wonderful man and I am blessed to call you my husband, my love and my friend.

Corbin--you are a special gift from God.

Kimberly--your continued encouragement for focus and direction will always be invaluable.

Springs Group Publishing--you put the wheels on this project and made my dream a reality!

> Jeff--my encounter with such an amazing marketing mind at the coffee shop gave me hope that this dream would be fulfilled.

> Jay-your enthusiasm, help and support for getting this project to press is a great encouragement.

Follow Me!

Find more information about Alane Pearce at:
www.notesfromthemarginsbook.com
and sign up to join the conversations on her blog

You can also become a fan of Alane Pearce at
facebook.com/home.php#/pages/Alane-
Pearce/77294696436

Or follow Alane on Twitter at
twitter.com/alanepearce

Order the companion Bible study

Comparing Notes:
a study of God's presence in our trials

on Amazon.com

In loving memory of

Andrew Holcombe Pearce
and all my kids
waiting for me in heaven

Table of Contents

A blessing for you
as you prepare for this journey:

Psalm 20

May the Lord answer you when you are in distress;
    may the name of the God of Jacob protect you.
May he send you help from the sanctuary and grant you
    support from Zion.
May he remember all your sacrifices and accept your burnt
    offerings.
May he give you the desire of your heart and make all your
    plans succeed.
We will shout for joy when you are victorious
    and we will lift up our banners in the name of our
    God.
May the Lord grant all your requests.

Now I know that the Lord saves his anointed,
    he answers him from his holy heaven
    with the saving power of his right hand.
Some trust in chariots and some in horses,
    but we trust in the name of the Lord our God.
They are brought to their knees and fall, but we rise up and
    stand firm.

Introduction

- Two parents stand over a baby in the neo-natal intensive care unit praying his fragile life be spared...***Does God hear?***
- A woman lies in bed, the weight of emotion bearing down on her so strongly that the thought of putting feet to the floor is too overwhelming...***Does God see?***
- Someone is tossing and turning at night; she is desperately trying to make sense of this trial life has dealt her; she seeks understanding in light of what she knows about God's character but the answer doesn't come...***Does God care?***

These are hard situations; hard questions. Questions we have all asked at one time or another. Maybe they are the same questions you are asking right now. There aren't easy answers, but there is comfort from God in times like these.

Through ten years of trials and devastating loss, and after many conversations with God, I've learned to trust that He never changes; He's the same yesterday, today and forever (Hebrews 13:8). He is there in the midst of our pain, waiting for us to call to Him. He longs to be our Rescuer; he desires to guide us through the pain. He wants us to find him and has given us the best roadmap to his heart; the Bible.

The words in the Bible are the words that heal, comfort, direct and forewarn those who have loved God since the beginning of time. Those very words can do the same for you and me when we choose to turn to God in our times of suffering. His living word, as applicable today as it was centuries ago, is one of the reasons my Bible is precious to me.

The pages of my Bible are tear-stained, wrinkled and worn, but I don't want a new one. This one has been with me through a heart-wrenching journey of growth. The notes in the margins of this dear book mark my journey through the pain of life. They record when my heart and soul were quickened by his word—when God whispered them just for me. They also mark the times God comforted, encouraged or warned me. Sometimes the notes are admonition to get my eyes back on God. They all note God's messages to me as he molds me into the image of Christ. This is a chronicle of those messages from God in a time of my greatest need— when it was just God and me walking through the valley of the shadow of death. There were so many times I just wanted to lie down and let the rain and darkness cover me up. There were times when I could not take another step because I was so tired of fighting.

There were times when it was a miracle that I actually took a step. These were the times when, as a friend of mine put it, I wanted to "pitch my tent and stay there." I didn't want to go any further; I just wanted to stop. Stop hurting. Stop living. Stop trusting in God. However, that is not what God wanted. He does not want any of us to stay in the darkness of the valley, no matter the circumstance. He longs to be gracious to you (Isaiah 30:18). He chases away the darkness with his light (John 8:12). He desires for us to know him and trust him (John 10:38).

Words like these kept me moving forward despite the agony. God's words healed my spirit, kept me on track and comforted my broken heart.

This is not a just book on infertility. It is not just a book on losing a child. Nor is it a book only about depression. This is a book about overcoming crises in life. We all have them, big and small. A crisis is something that is too hard to handle by ourselves, a circumstance that forces us to decide whether we want to wither in our own strength or call on the strength of God Almighty and trust that he can show us a way through it.

My crises happened to be losing a child, facing three emergency life-saving surgeries, suffering miscarriages, and battling depression. Your crisis may be similar, but more likely different: Supporting a family member with chronic illness, suffering a divorce, dealing with financial problems, infidelity, loneliness, losing a job—the list is never-ending. No matter what the crisis, if we trust in God to get us through it, he is faithful to answer our cries.

There is a lot of suffering in our world, but I do not think that is what God wants for us. His word clearly says that he came so we might have abundant life in Him (John 10:10). He does warn us of trouble but promises that he will provide refuge (Psalm 9:9). He wants us to have joy. He does not want us to reside in the darkness, lest we become adjusted to it. He doesn't want us to stay in the desert, lest we get used to it. He wants us to live in him and look forward to eternal life in his presence.

Follow as I recount the move out of the valley of my grief. Your valley may be similar and this story may help you, or it may help you better understand a friend's crisis. Open your heart and allow God to speak to you as he did to me.

Chapter One
An Accidental Journal

*T*he LORD gave me this answer: "Write down clearly on tablets what I reveal to you, so that it can be read at a glance." Habakkuk 2:2

You are either a note taker or you're not. I am. I like the reinforcement of writing something down to help commit it to memory or personality. My notes help me remember things; appointments, tasks, calls. They are written on scratch paper and sticky notes strewn around my life—in books or in the car, on my desk, the kitchen table and my night stand. They are almost too pervasive, but they keep me on track.

I also keep notes in a journal. Not every day, but when life is good and when life is hard. These notes help me see the path my life is on; they help me see where I've come from, how I've grown, and why I have the strength to face the next trial or a reason to celebrate the next joy. These notes are usually prayers or sometimes just observations, but they help keep me grounded. They make evident God's hand on my life.

Similarly, I keep notes in my Bible. Some of them are on old church bulletins or scraps of paper stuck here and there between the pages of this precious book. But most of the notes in my Bible are notes written in the margin.

These are records of the times in my life when I have hurled questions at God in the midst of a trial, or felt direction from him in the form of comfort, peace or even discipline.

These notes in the margins are spiritual markers in my life—a journal of sorts; conversations between God and me. They remind me of how real God is and how much he loves me. They help me see his leading and understand his will. They have kept me on track (or brought me back on track) when life became so difficult and so dark that I wasn't sure if I'd be able to take the next step.

Over the years, these notes in the margins have helped me see God's mercy in my grief, his willingness to listen to and answer hard questions, and his unwillingness to accept sinful and worldly behavior. Above all, they have helped me see glimpses of God's magnificent and profound character. It is through these conversations with God, recorded in the margins of my Bible, that I learned how to have joy instead of sorrow, and beauty instead of ashes.

There was a five-year period in my life when trial, grief and personal loss piled upon each other in a way that would cause a sensible person to crumble beneath it. I almost did. I couldn't understand why these things were happening to me. I questioned God's wisdom in all of it. I asked for help from my doctors—either I wasn't forceful enough or they did not understand what I was asking for—but I didn't get what I needed. It seemed like no one could really help me get through my grief and trials. So I turned to God.

When I did, he was faithful to meet me on the pages of my Bible. He comforted me with his words and gave me prayers when I had none. He was my counselor and my therapy. He directed me through my grief and back into his arms. The notes I share with you in this book are really my personal therapy sessions with God; they commemorate the tears, the trials, the lessons and finally the joys. Even today, the notes from these conversations with God encourage me and remind me how faithful he is.

Maybe you are a Bible note-taker, recording the events of your life in the pages of God's words. If you are, I am certain that your notes are precious to you. If you are not a note taker, I encourage to you become one. You will learn more about yourself, your God and your purpose when you take notes on your life. The notes in the margins of our Bibles—and our lives—can have enduring significance.

I was discussing the idea for this book with some friends whom I met at a retreat. One woman, Janice, was obviously moved as she listened. Later, she pulled me aside and shared a beautiful story about the notes in the margins of a Bible very precious to her. She said:

"My father died a few years ago after a fight with cancer. I struggled with so many hard questions about my faith when he died. I wondered why God took him so early, so quickly. One day, a verse from Romans was very heavy on my heart. I took out my new Bible—Dad's old one—and turned to the passage. When I saw the verse, I was struck by the words—not just the words of healing that came from God, but the words that were written in my fathers hand in the margin! I was so lonely for him, and these words were directly from him, as if he was sitting right with me consoling me. Those notes were powerful and so comforting."

I have other friends who are note-takers. Some of them have just started taking notes in their Bibles in a quest for a deeper relationship with God; others do it to learn how to apply the Bible to life. Some have taken notes in their Bibles when they were younger, in college for example, but have stopped.

I asked one friend, Mary, why she stopped taking notes on her life.

"I don't know," she admitted. "I guess I just got busy with kids and all." Then she paused for a long time. I asked if she was seeing how God was leading her now as well as she saw him back when she took life notes.

"I don't think so," she replied. "I mean, I know I'm still growing in my relationship, but I wouldn't be able to tell you how…maybe it's time to start noticing again," she added thoughtfully. "I can see how far I've come since I first made notes in the margins. And that's good. But maybe it's something to consider."

Maybe it is something for us all to consider. When we write down what God is doing in our lives, it is easier to see the path he is leading us on, and it's easier to see his hand in our lives. Sometimes I don't understand the long-term significance of some of my notes until years after I've written them. Surely, what I wrote was important to me at the time, but further down the road I have had new revelations about an old note or the verse that inspired it. I'll share an example.

In the book of Jeremiah in my worn out old Bible, there is a note in the margin by verse 11 in chapter 29. It reads: prayer verse for baby. The verse may be a familiar one: "For I know the plans I have for you," declares the Lord, "plans to prosper you and not harm you, plans to give you hope and a future." All these years I have been puzzled by that verse; it did not seem to fit the outcome of that particular pregnancy. There certainly wasn't hope or a future for my son who was born with a severe heart defect and lived for only 15 days.

Whenever I looked at that verse in the context of my note, I was sad and angry, even confused. I lived for years wondering what God had in mind when he laid that verse so heavily on my heart. He didn't answer me until I was ready to listen. It took eleven years.

Now there is a new note by that verse. It marks the time when God finally answered my lingering question. I was in the midst of a study on God's plans for us and Jeremiah 29:11 was part of the reading. I tried to read it with fresh eyes while

I pondered my note from years earlier. *"So much has happened in the eleven years since I was first pregnan*t," I thought. *"I have overcome so much; so many trials, losses and bouts of depression. Now thankfully here I am, finally living life free from bitterness and overwhelming grief. I do feel blessed."* And that is when I heard it. The Spirit whispered the message God wanted me to hear all along: "I know the plans I have for you; plans to prosper you and not harm you, plans to give you hope and a future." *That verse was for me all along!* the new note in the margin reads. "It was for me!" I shouted aloud. "It was for me."

That verse was for me!

Indeed, God has been faithful to give me hope and a future. He has used the many trials in my life to grow me and shape me into the woman he wants me to be. The notes in the margins of my Bible prove that. Those notes brought me healing when nothing else could; healing and help from the Great Physician, My Helper. The notes, inspired by God's word, help me remember where I've been and where he wants me to go for the very future and hope he told me of eleven years ago.

If you are facing a time of great need and you don't know where to turn, read on and discover for yourself the healing messages of God. I pray that you will be encouraged and comforted by them; that you will find healing for old wounds and freedom from grief, depression and captivity. God wants that for you!

Some of the lessons or conversations in this book may not make sense to you if you have never come to a saving knowledge of Jesus Christ. If you have not turned to Him for the cleansing of sin, you cannot easily understand how he could heal your pain. The truths in this book may not be relevant unless you draw near to him and trust him with your eternal fate.

If you have never believed in your heart and confessed with your mouth that Jesus Christ is the Lord (Romans 10:9), if you have never trusted that his death on the cross was payment for your sins and the restoration of your relationship with God, stop right now. Seek God through the blood shed on the cross for you. Pray this simple prayer, confess your sin and ask Jesus to cleanse your heart. You cannot be truly free until you do.

Dear Jesus,

I know that there is sin in my life and I know that this sin separates me from God. I don't want that; I want to be a child of God. I want to be free from my sin. I ask Jesus to come into my heart. I accept his free gift of salvation that he gave because of the cross. I accept that his blood has covered my sins and that my life will be changed by his love. Thank you, Jesus, for hearing my prayer. Thank you for giving me eternal life. Fill me with your Spirit and teach me what it means to have new life in You. Amen

Chapter Two:
Days of Darkness

*L*ight is sweet and it pleases the eyes to see the sun. However many years a man may live, let him enjoy them all. But let him remember the days of darkness, for they will be many. Ecclesiastes 11:7-8

The days of darkness do seem like many, many unending days of pain and grief. Especially when you are in the midst of those dark days; when you can't get out of bed when life is bearing down hard on you because just the thought of standing up exhausts you. When the trials and the pain and grief wear on and it feels like it will never stop; like you will never be able to breathe normally, or laugh for the rest of your life.

This kind of darkness can overtake you. It can hide the sunshine and the joy of life until you think it must be God's will for you to suffer. Therefore, you keep walking in the dark because you no longer know what else to do. Eventually, you become accustomed to the darkness and that's where you stay because you have forgotten that it does not have to be that way. This is how my life was from the time I was 28 until after I turned 39. Dark. Burdensome. Tiring. Confusing. I suffered an immeasurable series of losses and grief which overtook me, skewing my faith and confusing my perspective.

Brandon and I had been married for two years when we decided it was time to start a family. After all, we had plants we kept alive, and even a dog had survived our trial run of caring for something beyond ourselves. We thought we passed some kind of "pre-parenting test," so having children was the obvious next step for us. Little did we know the plans God had for us. Even as I write this, I have to remind myself that those plans are for good, not harm. Now I can see some of the good God brought out of his plans and our trials. In the midst of them, I couldn't.

I can still remember the day I found out I was pregnant. I thought I was, but I wasn't sure. I took a home test and it registered a light positive. *Maybe it's still early*, I thought. Secretly, I started making plans; decorating a nursery in my head, picking out names, slowing down through the baby isle at the store. I looked at all the pink and blue outfits, towels, bibs and jammies. *What will I need?* I thought. *What kind of names go with Pearce?*

It was only a week later when Brandon and I faced our first loss; a ruptured tubal pregnancy that almost took my life. I was talking with some friends in the hallway of our church in Hawaii (during our most exotic tour with the Air Force) when I felt a sharp pain in my side followed by a gush of blood. *I guess I'm not pregnant,* I thought to myself. *I'm starting my period after all.* After I told Brandon the news, I sat on the couch for the rest of the day lamenting that getting pregnant was harder than I thought. We had been trying for five months, and still nothing.

The next morning, I was getting ready for my day. Brandon had come in at 6:00 a.m. from his overnight shift and stumbled into bed. The shift work did not bother him too much, once he was in bed he could sleep through a tornado.

I was drying my hair when I doubled over from a sharp pain in my side. I thought I would throw up and pass out at the time. I have a high tolerance for pain, but this was like nothing I'd ever felt before. I made my way to the other side of the house so if I did get sick, it wouldn't concern Brandon. When I made it to the other bathroom, I fell to the cold linoleum floor sweating and crying, barely able to breathe. All I could say was, *Jesus, help me! Jesus, help me!* I knew this was serious and I needed help fast but I couldn't move for the pain.

Suddenly, it felt as if someone lifted me and helped me crawl back to my bedroom. I couldn't raise my voice, but I was saying in a loud whisper, "Brandon, help me!" Miraculously, Brandon woke up from a sound sleep and carried me to the bed. He lifted the phone to call 911.

"Don't call the ambulance; I don't want everyone to know!" I complained.

"There's nothing else I can do, honey," Brandon, ever rational in an emergency, calmly replied.

The EMTs were nearly as baffled as we were at first because there were no external signs of bleeding, but my blood pressure was dangerously low. "Must be gas," one said. "It will pass."

"She usually doesn't pass out from gas," Brandon said.

"Could she be pregnant?" another asked.

"We thought she was," replied Brandon.

That's when the medical team raced into action. They guessed that the fetus had lodged in one of my fallopian tubes and as it grew, it ruptured the tube and tore a major vein. I was bleeding out in my abdomen.

We were living in a house built in the 1930's and the gurney wouldn't fit through the doors, so the technicians quickly made a sling with some blankets and rolled me into it. I screamed with pain whenever they moved me. Once I was in the ambulance, the driver drove as slowly as he could as they transported me to Tripler Army Medical Center, the big pink hospital on a hill above Honolulu. About five miles from the ER, my blood pressure crashed again and the driver flipped on the emergency lights and sped me up the hill. I can only imagine what Brandon must have thought as he followed in our car.

When I arrived in the ER, I was in shock from losing so much blood, which was pooling in my abdominal cavity. My stomach was distended from the pressure of the blood and I was shaking with cold, despite the five layers of warmed blankets piled on my body and around my head.

As I lay on the gurney waiting for the surgeons to prep, I looked up and saw Brandon's worried face silently praying over me. We both thought that I might die and a sense of sobriety came over me.

"Brandon," I whispered. "Know that I love you."

"I love you, too," he choked as a tear slipped from his eye.

"If something happens, I don't want any extreme attempts to save my life," I told him. "I want a living will so you won't have to make those choices."

Brandon looked over and said something to the doctors.

"We don't have time to make a living will," said one of the talking heads above me.

"Let's just make an Officer's agreement between the three of us (all Air Force or Army Officers) that we won't make any Herculean attempts to save her life," said the other head.

I felt Brandon's hand slip from mine and saw the tiles on the ceiling rush by as they wheeled me to the operating room.

The last thing I remember from that day was the oxygen mask being placed over my face and someone saying, "Now you might feel some pressure." In my irrational state of mind, I was afraid I would suffocate because I couldn't feel the air they were giving me. It was all they could do to keep me from pulling the mask off my face. They strapped my arms down and I was out.

When I woke up in the intensive care unit, I was actually a little disappointed. The last thing I thought before surgery was, *"Well, if I have to go through this, it would be cool to see a glimpse of heaven."* I didn't see a glimpse. Not even a hint of a shiny light, an angel or familiar face. I just remember "feeling a little pressure" and then waking up hearing a song playing over the radio I hadn't heard since I was a child: *My name is Michael, I have a nickel. I have a nickel all shiny and new. I'm gonna use it to buy me some candy. That's what I'm gonna do...* The 1970's hit by Clint Holmes echoed in the back of my mind. I took a trip back to my childhood when my sisters and I happily sang the chorus of that song in the back of our International TravelAll on our way to various camping sites across the west. That was a time of joyous freedom from life's worries.

Finally, I opened my eyes and was swiftly ushered to the present as I saw Brandon sitting by my bed holding my hand. I tried to talk to ask him how it went, but I couldn't. I still had the breathing tube down my throat. I started panicking the way I did in the ER—afraid I was going to suffocate because I couldn't feel fresh air. That set off a bunch of alarms and the nurses came running in the room. Brandon assured me they would take out the tube as soon as they could. That helped calm me down. He knew my greatest fear is suffocating and he tried to keep me distracted so I would relax.

It didn't occur to me until now, as I'm writing, all that my wonderful husband went through while he watched this happen to me. All the calls he made to friends, family and church, and all the time he spent waiting for news about my well-being, worrying that I might die.

Our marriage, which probably had the risk—at least statistically—of ending in divorce, grew so much stronger during our years of trial piled upon trial. It's easy to see now the evidence of how God was watching over us. Brandon learned (and remembers) to appreciate me for all the times he nearly lost me, and I've remembered to lean on him and let him help me through the rough times. So many times, if he was having a hard time coping with our stresses, I was doing well and could help him out of his pit. Other times, if I was having a bad day (he could just look at me and know), he'd take action to help pick me up. We grew together and closer to God which strengthened us for the trials to follow.

The rest of my stay in the ICU is a blur. I was sleeping a lot and I always felt bad because Brandon was there and I thought I should be talking with him. I often drifted off in the middle of our conversations, but I always loved waking up and seeing him there.

I was in the hospital for a little over a week. After they moved me from the ICU to a regular ward, I had the time and strength to think about what happened. This was the first incident in what I now know would be a long series of losing eight children. At this point, I didn't even question my faith or God's hand on my life. I figured it happened for a reason and frankly, I was so happy to be alive that it really didn't matter *why*. We could still easily see God's hand in our circumstances.

One day on his way to the hospital for his daily visit, Brandon saw a large ball of paper lying in the gutter. Thinking it looked like a wad of money, he turned the car around at the next light, only half expecting it to still be in the street. He parked the car and to both of our surprise he picked up a stack of $120 in ones and fives. He asked around to see if anyone had dropped it, and no one claimed it, so he did. Interestingly, the hospital bill and all the food he bought while there totaled almost $120. We knew God was watching out for us.

Before I was released from the hospital, the doctors made sure I knew what happened; they performed an emergency Laparotomy where they cut me from navel to pelvis and removed a portion of the offending fallopian tube. When they cut me open, one doctor said a red fountain gushed out of my abdomen—I had lost half of my blood! They also gave me a blood transfusion, which they said would take four or five months to recover from since they didn't have time to match my blood type.

After I came home from the hospital, all I could do was sleep. Our friends from church and Brandon's work brought meals, called and sent cards, which was a great blessing and another of the ways God provided for us. Brandon took time off from work to nurse me back to health and walk me around the block every day.

The first time we went outside, I was so overwhelmed by the lush, bright colors of the flowers and the beautiful shades of green in the grasses and plants. It was as if God had given me new eyes to appreciate his creation. My eyes grew dim again all too quickly which made me wonder…do newborn babies have that great wonder with freshly created eyes from God? What causes them to dim so quickly? How could I hold on to that awe and wonder that was so overwhelming after I had nearly died?

It was a grueling two months recovering from this surgery. The five-inch incision on my stomach looked like a train track from the staples every two centimeters. It was painful to sit or move and I took a long time to heal. Summer ended by the time I had the energy to make it through the day without sleeping. Fall began in the world and in my life.

In October, the doctor cleared my health and Brandon and I tried to get pregnant again. By Christmas we announced to our family and friends that we were indeed having a successful pregnancy and in January, Brandon left for a short tour of duty in Saudi Arabia. I sent him pictures of my growing belly and described in letters how incredible it was to have a life growing in me.

It was actually quite a normal pregnancy, and even though I was experiencing it alone while my husband served across the world, I was never happier. All my life I wanted to have babies and be a mom. I never remember wanting to do anything else. I couldn't help thinking that all my dreams, goals and ambitions would be completed in this child.

While Brandon was gone, I immersed myself in Bible study, wanting to know God better in the hope of preparing for motherhood. In March of that year I read, for maybe the first time, Jeremiah 29:11-14—the verse I discussed earlier. I began praying this every day for the baby within me, knowing that God honors our devotion and his word, but never really seeing that those words were actually for me.

In May, further on in my Bible study, I read the books of First and Second Peter in my devotional times. That was when I read a note in the margin of the page that I had made almost a year earlier. It was simply a date on the page by 1 Peter 1:3-8.

> Praise be to the God and Father of our Lord Jesus Christ! In his great mercy he has given us new birth into a living hope through the resurrection of Jesus Christ from the dead and into an inheritance that can never spoil or fade—kept in heaven for you, who through God's power until the coming of the salvation that is ready to be revealed in the last time. In this you greatly rejoice, though now for a little while you may have had to suffer grief in all kinds of trials. These have come so that your faith—of greater worth than

gold, which perishes even though refined by fire—may be proved genuine and may result in praise, glory and honor when Jesus Christ is revealed.

God was trying to prepare me!

The date by that verse was four days before my tube burst and put me in peril nearly a year earlier.

God was trying to prepare me! I wrote that day. *He showed me this verse to strengthen me right before I needed it. I wish I had paid attention to it then,* I thought.

This was a pivotal moment; it had all just come together for me. If I continue to seek God in his word, then he will prepare me for the things he asks me to do. I searched this idea a little further and found in Genesis where God wondered aloud whether he should tell Abraham what he planned for Sodom and Gomorrah. He did. Then I looked at the Old Testament prophets and saw how God told his people exactly what would happen if they obeyed and if they disobeyed. In the New Testament, I found even Jesus often told his disciples what would happen next. Nobody understood those divine messages at the time, just as I didn't understand my "heads up" from God. Nonetheless, I was told so I would be prepared.

I decided that I didn't want to miss any more messages from God so I started marking dates and notes in my Bible whenever I was spiritually impressed by a sermon, a message or by my own study. I started journaling as well. I wanted to see where God was leading. Wisely, he never told me exactly what he was going to ask of me until it was time for me to do it. I think if he did, I would have refused to walk through that valley and thereby miss a deeper dimension to my faith. I would have missed a lot of pain and the shedding of gallons of tears as well; I would have liked to miss that.

My notes were sporadic, but I was laying down a habit that would be the key to getting me through the coming difficult years. I had started counseling appointments, if you will, with the Lord Almighty who counseled me with wisdom and love, giving me everything I needed at the proper time.

Summer approached and I felt the same as the season; happy and carefree. My pregnancy was progressing well, my husband was due back from the Middle East and we were opening our home to some missionaries coming to work on our church.

Brandon came home the day before terrorists bombed Kobar Towers in Saudi Arabia. We felt quite blessed because that is where Brandon stayed the night before he flew out of the country. Three days later, another bomb hit. This time it was in my abdomen. Again.

I had been cleaning the house for our company and I suddenly became quite sore in my stomach, then a nauseous feeling rose up from my chest. I thought I had just cleaned too hard and my 28-week pregnancy was telling me to slow down. When Brandon came home from running some errands, he found me on the bed in pain.

We decided to go to the hospital, and since I was so far along, I had to report to labor and delivery. I could hardly walk down the hall. One lady, clearly at the end of her pregnancy, looked at me and said, "Oh, you lucky!" thinking I was in labor. "I don't think its good news," I managed to reply.

It wasn't good news. It took the doctors hours to figure out what was wrong. First, they determined that nothing was wrong with the baby and that whatever was happening to me wasn't affecting him. My temperature was only 95 degrees and I was dripping wet with sweat as if I'd just been in the bath.

"Why are you so wet?" the technician asked as he prepared to take an ultrasound.

"Maybe it's one of the clues that something is wrong," I sarcastically suggested.

After four hours, they suspected my appendix ruptured so they admitted me and scheduled surgery for later that night. They took me into a labor room and strapped me to IVs and machines to monitor both the baby and me. They tried drawing blood and poked me several times on each arm, each hand and each foot to no avail. They finally strapped me down on the bed insuring that I wouldn't move, and took the necessary blood from my jugular vein.

It took me a long time to recover from that surgery because my appendix had indeed ruptured, spreading infection throughout my body. They had to leave the incision open and clean it out every day. They gave me so many drugs and antibiotics that they needed two IV trees to hang everything. In addition, my body was trying to force the baby out so the doctors added pitocin to keep me from going into labor and strapped me to monitors to watch the baby. Let me tell you, getting up to use the rest room was an event! I should have been in the intensive care unit, but they kept me in labor and delivery to protect the baby.

I was not allowed to walk or move much because it could have triggered labor. As a result, I developed horrible bedsores and my intestinal tract paralyzed. One morning I laid my hand on my belly and heard the sound of a drum echoing from my stomach. When the doctor came in for his rounds, I played him a tune on my tummy. When I asked him if that was supposed to happen, he freaked out because the stomach gasses had built up in my belly and had no place to go. My middle was quite distended, although it was difficult to tell because of the pregnancy, and the doctor was afraid that my stomach would burst. They quickly went to work shoving a nasal-gastro-intestinal tube (NG Tube) up my nose and down my throat.

This was the worst thing I ever endured—even worse than my ruptured tube the year earlier, and anything that has happened since! I have a horrible gag reflex and it took them a half hour just to get the small tube down my throat. They made me sip water and each time I swallowed, they pushed the tube further into my esophagus—about a centimeter at a time. It upset me so much that my throat constricted, which complicated the process. Once in place, the tube released the gasses in my intestinal tract and suctioned out foul smelling green goo as well. I felt so gross that I wouldn't let anyone come see me during the eight days I was confined to that labor and delivery bed.

I learned that week that I am allergic to the tape they used to secure my IV, heart monitor and baby monitors. I had red-hot blisters everywhere the tape touched my skin. They stuck to the tape when they removed it, leaving raw sores on my arms and chest.

The nurses felt so sorry for me. One of them searched the whole hospital until she found an "egg crate" mattress topper to help relieve me of the pressure points and pain from the bedsores, and another would come in every day to brush and braid my dirty, greasy hair.

The room had no windows and no TV (until they finally brought me one on a cart that received one channel). That week the station ran a continuous marathon of *Waterworld*. I actually saw the whole movie once or twice in the bits and pieces I caught between my sleep all that week.

I would often wake up hearing screams from other women in labor which added an eerie psychic ward feeling to my experience. Sometimes during the night, I saw a shadow behind my door, which they usually left open, that resembled a tall hooded man whom I supposed was Death. I wondered if he was waiting for me.

I watched the shadow and considered death. Was I ready to die? Was everything in order? I had no ill will with family. Brandon and I were fine. There was nothing left undone except being a mom. I decided I was okay with dying if that was my fate. I wasn't even afraid because since I had accepted Jesus as my Savior, I knew I would be with him in heaven. That certainly had to be better than what I was going through. It turned out that death would have a different appointee later that year.

I was quite relieved when after a week they removed the NG Tube and moved me to a regular ward with a regular bed, a window and a TV with more programming than *Waterworld*. After four more days, I went home with instructions to shower twice a day to clean the three-inch open sore on the right side of my stomach. It was all I could manage to do between my naps.

Again, our friends at church sent cards and meals and helped whenever they could and we managed to get through the rest of the summer with help from our family and friends. For the most part, I lay on the couch, waited for my due date, and made grand plans in my head of our new life with a baby. My best friends, who were both pregnant as well, would talk about fitting three highchairs around a Thanksgiving table, and the fun things we would do during the Christmas holidays. We planned play dates (more for us than the babies), and trips to the beach. We knew our times together on Hawaii would give us amazing memories of friendship and fun.

In the meantime, my mid-August due date came and went. My mom arrived to help me out and we hoped she'd be able to see the baby before her plane left for the mainland in 10 days.

A week after I was due, I had a regular check up that turned into another hospital stay. (This one has a happy ending!) My doctor was concerned that I had lost my amniotic fluid and admitted me to the hospital so they could induce labor. I was quite put out because, being a new Mom, I had a labor bag with "everything I'd need" waiting for me at home but the doctor would not let me leave. My mom called Brandon who came straight to the hospital from work.

The rest of that day is a blur of pain and joy. I had back labor which was extremely painful and intensified from the labor-inducing drugs. Brandon rubbed my back, trying to offer me comfort, but he would sometimes fall asleep on the job since it was approaching midnight and he had been up since five a.m.

Finally, well after midnight on August 30th, the baby crowned, but naturally there were complications—I just can't seem to do anything the easy way!

Suddenly the nurses were unplugging me from the machines in the labor room, whisking me down the hallway to the surgical ward, and telling me not to push. I was desperately trying to remember what I learned in childbirth classes when I was quickly ushered in surgery where they used forceps and then a vacuum to pull our son, Andrew, into the world. --

Then they laid him on my chest. I have never been happier. All my purpose, hopes and dreams rested in my arms that very moment. I looked at this little boy, with his big bright brown eyes looking back at me, and I was overcome with awe, and overwhelming love.

When they brought Andrew to me the next morning, the poor little guy had bruises on his hands and feet. "Hard to get his blood," the nurse hastily explained. "He's breathing fast," another noted when she came to take his pulse. I held him and tried to nurse him; I took tons of pictures and marveled at this little creation.

Before they released us from the hospital, they made an appointment to follow up for jaundice. "He's just a little yellow," the doctor said. If I had any medical training, I might have guessed that something was amiss with all of these little problems.

The first day at home, Andrew was an angel; he didn't cry, he loved to be held and he didn't even mind the dog's big nose in his face. We kept him under lights for his jaundice and took him for a quick walk around the block hoping the sunlight would help his liver. The second day he was home he got fussy; colic, we all assumed. I noticed he was breathing faster and I was wondering why. Even my mother didn't know. I called the nurse hot line and they didn't seem very concerned, but suggested I check back with my doctor.

By the third day, Andrew was noticeable lethargic. His breathing was labored and he would no longer nurse. We panicked. "*Lord, please tell us what to do,*" we prayed. I was happy my mom was there helping Brandon and me make decisions we've never had to face before. We decided to take him to the hospital.

We drove to the ER, a drive with which my husband was becoming all too familiar. This was Andrew's last ride in a car, the last time he'd see our house and the last time we would hold him without worrying about wires and tubes.

When we arrived at the ER, they took me and Andrew right in. They later said he was a textbook case for hypo plastic left heart, a severe heart defect where the left side of the heart is too hardened to flex and therefore unable to pump oxygenated blood through his little body. This was why he was breathing quickly and why the nurses couldn't get blood from him very easily when he was first born. After a child is born, it takes about three or four days for this condition to show up, and Andrew was right on schedule.

He was so dehydrated when he came to the ER that they couldn't get an IV in him. Instead, they put a shunt into his shin so they could hydrate him through his marrow. I stood back in shock. Who knew my baby was this sick?

Brandon joined me in the ER room and questions flooded our minds; *Why is this happening? What does it mean? Will he be okay? What caused this? What do we do now?* We never saw any of this coming.

We waited out the night in the waiting room of the pediatric intensive care unit (PICU) where the nurses brought us blankets and pillows and let us see Andrew for 5 minutes every hour. Our pastor and close friends came to visit. There was one time, early in the morning, when there were no other people in the waiting room except for Brandon, my mom and me that an elderly couple walked in and approached us.

"Can we pray for you?" they asked.

"YES!" I responded, ready to tell them about our baby in the PICU. Before I could, they sat and held our hands and the man began praying. I don't remember what he said, but I am still moved by the picture of them coming to pray with us and knowing what to pray. Then they left and we never saw them again. I wonder to this day if they were angels sent by God to assure us he was still there.

Here is where the story gets hard. Even now, eleven years after it happened, I struggle through writing this. I wonder if it's more than a coincidence that the week I write this part of the story is the anniversary of Andrew's birthday and his short life.

After two days at the hospital in Hawaii, we were told they needed to move Andrew to Children's Hospital in San Diego because hey didn't have enough of the medication he needed and since we were on an island, they couldn't get any quick enough. They were flying out another family who had a baby with a heart defect and wanted to add us to that flight. We had two hours to get our affairs together.

God is in control

We mobilized our friends to help us pack and take care of the house and the dog. Our pastor and Sunday school gathered around us for prayer. The song, "God is in Control" ran through my head. Not really the song, just that phrase…*God is in control.*

The plane was a big military transport that held a crew, a nurse and doctor team, two incubators, the other couple and us. On board, Brandon and I prayed. We prayed together and we prayed silently. There wasn't much else to do in the cavernous belly of the plane—it had no seats (just mesh benches), no movies, no peanuts or pretzels. Just some parents and our very sick babies flying over the Pacific Ocean. It seemed to take forever to get to San Diego.

We were in what I've come to call Survival Mode; a state of mental anguish that allows you to robot your way through a situation without emotion or feeling, to accomplish the task in the most detached way possible. I kept my distance from the incubator because I thought, "What if he dies; it will be harder to handle if I'm attached to him." So I stayed detached.

All the while, the words "God is in control" played in my head. I even told Brandon that I knew Andrew would be all right because God is in control. After all, we were Christians, followers of Jesus. As such, we are God's adopted children. Isn't God supposed to take care of His children? Isn't He supposed to save them? Doesn't He make everything okay?

Years earlier, when I read and understood the story of Abraham in the Bible, I had always wondered if I'd be brave enough to give up my son to God's will. Now here I was, facing that very test—wanting to be strong but really, I was scared and full of questions.

At the hotel that night, after we made sure Andrew was okay in the Neo-Natal Intensive Care Unit (NICU) at Children's Hospital in our new temporary home of San Diego, Brandon and I prayed again. This time we told God, "We lay Andrew on your altar, knowing that you are a good and gracious God. We know Your ways are better than ours are. We know you are wise beyond our imagination. We give you Andrew and we ask you to heal him according to your will."

The next week was full of long days in waiting rooms punctuated by visits with Andrew and phone calls to friends and family. The doctor wanted to postpone surgery until Andrew's liver and kidneys recovered since we was so close to death earlier that week. Both of our families came out to be with us offering their support, and a local pastor who was friends with our friends from Hawaii, tracked us down and sat with us. We finally started to hold Andrew as much as we could.

My mom actually changed my mind about bonding with him. She said, "Honey, if something does happen to him and you didn't take the time God has given you with him, you will regret it deeply. Don't let your fear of losing him keep you from loving him." Wise advice.

The nurses noted how Andrew's heart rate and other stats normalized whenever we held him. They took great pains to prepare a chair for us close enough for the wires and tubes extruding from his head and arms to reach. They even recommended we read some stories and sing some songs onto a tape recorder which they played for him in our absence. We did everything we could to be there for him. I even gave him his first sponge bath which he wasn't happy about at all! I hoped and prayed that this was not the only bath I'd be able to give our son.

Finally, the day for his heart surgery arrived. This was the first of a series of at least three surgeries Andrew would have had over his lifetime. Each surgery had a fifty percent chance of survival. Each day between the surgeries also held a fifty percent chance of survival. This first surgery would take eight hours for the doctors to put a shunt in his heart to allow the oxygenated blood to pump through his right ventricle instead of his left. They took out one of the arteries in his left arm to accomplish this task. His heart was only the size of the tip of an adult's thumb. I was amazed that the surgeons could work on such a small organ.

I have this next memory etched so deeply in my head; it was the last time we saw or held Andrew when he was alive and alert. We held him and talked to him in "pre-op" and then we laid him in the clear plastic rolling bassinet which they used to transport him to surgery. As they rolled him away, Andrew caught my eyes with his big brown ones. He moved his head as they rolled him down the hall so he could look at me until they turned the corner. I wondered if he knew what was going on. I wished I could have told him that everything would be okay.

The next day we had the chance to see Andrew, but we couldn't touch him because he was on a paralytic drug to keep him still; any movement could affect his life.

After a short visit, the nurses in the NICU urged us to go out to dinner because there wasn't much we could do. After much coaxing from the nurses and Brandon, I reluctantly left the waiting room and headed for a dinner out. I called the NICU every 20 minutes to see how Andrew was doing—which was an expensive task in the days before cell phones. It was only when we went to bed that night that I actually stopped worrying about Andrew. He was nearly through the critical period of the first 36 hours from surgery. I was soon thanking God for bringing us as far as he had, and I drifted off to sleep.

The phone in our hotel room rang and I rubbed my eyes to see the time. It was 3:15 a.m. No good news comes in the middle of the night. Brandon picked up the phone with trepidation. Indeed, it was bad news. The night nurse at the NICU was reporting that Andrew's vitals were crashing and we needed to get to the hospital right away.

It seemed to take forever to get to the hospital; the taxi was slow to come and all the lights seemed to linger on red. It seemed like the whole world wanted to move in slow motion and I wanted to speed it all up. By the time we arrived at the hospital, Andrew was dead. They led us into the NICU to where his body lay. I could tell he wasn't just sleeping. He looked different without life.

My world fell apart. It felt like I slipped into a dark tunnel and I was plunging into an abyss. I could hardly breathe. I kept looking to Brandon to make him tell me why it happened. Why? It wasn't supposed to happen.

God was supposed to be in control…didn't that mean everything would be fine?

I finally understood the pictures you see of people throwing themselves on caskets. There is nothing else to do with the grief except collapse. But I didn't just collapse, I shut down.

Chapter Three
Existing Through the Grief

*H*e gives strength to the weary and increases the power of the weak. Even youths grow tired and weary, and young men stumble and fall; but those who hope in the Lord will renew their strength. They will soar on wings like eagles; they will run and not grow weary, they will walk and not be faint. Isaiah 41:29-31.

It turns out that shock and grief are actually wonderful gifts from God. When Andrew died, we were in a state of shock. Shock is God's way of keeping grief from killing you. Grief is an outlet for your emotions, but if the full load of grief hit you all at the same time, you wouldn't survive it. Praise God for the numbing effects of shock. As it was, my moribund hopes and dreams—my whole life even—were overcome by such darkness that it nearly suffocated me.

We were ushered into a private room next to the NICU where we held Andrew's body and said our good byes. There, our minds were bombarded by soul-wrenching questions: *Why would God let a baby die? It doesn't make sense. It's not fair. How do we reconcile this event with our life-long faith? What does this mean about God?* It took a very long time to answer these questions. Some of them still linger, but I'm okay with that now.

When Andrew turned cold, we gave him back to the nurses who assisted us with funeral arrangements, etc. Then we headed back to the hotel. We sat for a long time in our dark room. There was nothing left to say. I actually felt conflicted because I wanted to be there for my husband, but I needed my mommy who was waiting in her hotel room down the hall. We both agreed to be with our respective families who were there for us. I cried every time I tried to speak, so I just didn't bother talking anymore. I knocked on my mom's door and my sister opened it to me. I walked in and laid my head in my mommy's lap. I must have stayed that way for hours.

Eventually, she coaxed me into walking down to the café for a muffin and coffee. My mom actually ordered for me. I couldn't even make a decision about what to eat. Food seemed so stupid to me. I couldn't even taste it. Nothing mattered anymore.

Later, I met Brandon back in our room and he told me our friend's pastor was coming to see us. He thought that maybe I should at least comb my hair, so I made him come into the bathroom with me because I didn't want to be alone. I was afraid the darkness surrounding me would suffocate and crush me if someone wasn't nearby.

The pastor came to our room and took out his Bible. He turned to 2 Samuel 12:19-23. This is the account of David when his son from Bathsheba died as an infant. The pastor read aloud:

> David noticed that his servants were whispering among themselves and realized the child was dead. "Is the child dead?" he asked.
>
> "Yes," they replied, "he is dead."
>
> Then David got up from the ground. After he had washed, put on lotions and changed his clothes, he went into the house of the Lord and worshipped. Then he went to his own house, and at his request they served him food and he ate.
>
> His servants asked him, "Why are you acting this way? While the child was alive, you fasted and wept, but now that the child is dead, you get up and eat!"
>
> He answered, "While the child was still alive, I fasted and wept. I thought, 'Who knows? The Lord may be gracious to me and let the child live.' But now that

he is dead, why should I fast? Can I bring him back again? I will go to him, but he will not return to me.

You have to keep living

I was amazed at how the Bible seemed to have an answer for our situation. I noted in the margin of my Bible, *"You have to keep living"* and wrote how this verse helped me deal with Andrew's death. This was actually my first grief counseling session with God. Granted, the pastor read the verse and prayed, but it was God who taught me many things as I meditated on this verse for the rest of the day.

First, he gave me a plan to work through my grief; get up wash, dress, and do my hair and makeup—every day. For the first few months after Andrew died, I always considered it a good day if I could accomplish these things.

Next, the passage helped me understand that no amount of wishing, hoping or complaining would change the situation. Andrew was dead and there was nothing I could do about it. Nevertheless, there is hope that one day I will see him and know him for eternity because I know Jesus, and Andrew is with him.

Finally, both Brandon and I learned what we had to do next as together we pondered verse 20; "Then David got up from the ground. After he washed, put on lotions and changed his clothes, he went into the house of the Lord and worshipped." It's easy to worship God when life is sunny and fair, but here we were, as David was, deeply hurt by a confusing event in our lives. Worshipping God in the midst of this is truly a sacrifice. It is not easy to go to a God who just let your son die and say, "I love you and I trust you anyway."

Even though we were in no place to say that to God the day after Andrew died, we did choose to go to church to worship. The verse prompted us, but I think we really made the decision to go out of habit—it's what we've both always done. The next day, Sunday, we almost longed for church; not so much out of a desire for God but in need of the routine—something, anything to make life feel normal again. It felt weird to want to go to church when we were questioning God, but we thought it would be harder to deal with life without God, even when we didn't understand what he was doing. We did not want to turn our backs on him because we were longing for comfort and understanding. We wanted answers from him.

We yearned for our home church in Hawaii, where our friends would have met us and enveloped us in their love and sympathy; but we walked into another church in a strange city where, instead of our friends, God met us. He was in the people sitting around us who offered love without knowing our sorrow. He was in the songs the choir sang. He was in the sunshine streaming through the stained glass windows.

Just the ritual of being in church was comforting; much like slipping into a warm bath after a hard day. The songs sung of pain and redemption and the sermon spoke of love and mercy. I took a deep breath for the first time in 36 hours. I languished in the warmth of unconditional love and let it wash over my shock and sorrow—even if it was for just an hour.

Then something brought me back to the present and tears filled my eyes again. *Can this really be happening?* I asked myself. *All I ever wanted was to be a mom, and in a day, it has been ripped away. All I was living for is gone. What am I to do now?*

The choir caught my attention with "Because He Lives." I listened intently to the words; because Jesus lives, I can face tomorrow no matter what it brings. *Tomorrow is too far away,* I thought. *But maybe, just maybe, I can face today.* "...life is worth the living just because he lives," the choir finished.

I looked down and saw a brand new copy of *Our Daily Bread* sitting beside me. I reached for this little devotional out of curiosity. *What does is say about yesterday, September 14th, the day Andrew died?* I wondered.

I quickly found the page and read the verse; "Take this cup away from Me (Jesus prays); nevertheless, not what I will, but what you will" Mark 14:36. My heart quickened. God met me in this devotional as well. Hadn't I prayed for God's will to be done? Didn't I say I'd accept it? It was time to decide if I really meant what I said, or if I was just making a promise to God that I'd keep if things turned out the way *I* wanted them to.

These encounters with God in church on

September 15th were not an overnight cure to all the questions that plagued me, but they were a tiny step to recovering from my grief. God did meet me in church that day. He gave me the comfort I needed. Not my pastor, not my friends, but God himself. He gently held me in his arms while I struggled with him and grappled with my circumstances. He lovingly whispered in my ear, "Because Jesus lives, you will too. You *will live* through this. Trust in my love, child. Trust in my love."

I doubt I would have seen God so readily if we had been at our home church. I would have felt the love of our friends and pastor as we had through all of our trials to date. However, because we were in a church where no one new of our sorrow, and because we followed his leading, we found him ready to comfort us instead of our friends.

Even so, I felt like I was on a roller coaster. One minute I could rest in God and the next I was crying and mad at my circumstances.

We couldn't leave San Diego until Andrew's body was taken care of and ready for travel, so our families took us around the city and to the mall to distract us from our misery. It didn't work for me. I couldn't even go into the stores to shop because everything seemed so hopeless. I saw things that I had wanted to do or get for Andrew and I would fall into a heap crying. I would see other people with children and I'd want to scream out, "Why you and not me?! All I've ever wanted was to be a mommy and God took that away!"

Men and women grieve in such different ways. While I was struggling to make sense of life, Brandon could compartmentalize what had happened. Shopping and sightseeing distracted him enough to get some relief from his pain so he could help me through mine. I was grateful for that.

Five days after Andrew died, we headed back home to Hawaii with empty arms. It was horrible packing up Andrew's clothes, books and toys. It was hard checking the empty car seat/carrier we had packed for our trip home with Andrew. It was gut wrenching to be going home without our baby. I dreaded walking into our house and being there without him. I loathed the thought of putting away the nursery we had so lovingly prepared. (It actually took me almost a year to go in there again and then only because we were moving. I was thankful that the movers packed up the room for me.) In addition, I hated the idea of looking at a little casket during a funeral service.

I despised the thought of the funeral so much, that I wouldn't even plan it. I just wanted to pretend as if nothing happened. I was quite determined to avoid any kind of service, but my mother pointed out that my friends and family needed the funeral, and so did I. I relented to having a memorial service and my best friends in Hawaii planned every detail for me. All we had to do was find a verse to share. God showed us this:

> All this is for your benefit, so that the grace
> that is reaching more and more people

may cause thanksgiving to overflow to the glory of God. Therefore we do not lose heart. Though outwardly we are wasting away, yet inwardly we are being renewed day by day. For our light and momentary troubles are achieving for us an eternal glory that far outweighs them all. For what is seen is temporary, but what is unseen is eternal. 2 Corinthians 4:15-18

It struck me as an odd verse to share at the time, but we did it anyway feeling pressed by God to do so. It made more sense while watching the families in our church during the weeks after Andrew's funeral. I couldn't understand how my son's death would be for my benefit, but I did see the grace that touched our church and caused thanksgiving to overflow.

Instead of a funeral, I really wanted to give a testimony to the church holding my living son in my arms saying, "God heals and here's my proof!" Instead, the proof of God's healing and grace was in the moms and dads who held their children tighter. It was in the way they appreciated their families more as they realized, because of our loss, what a gift the life of a child was. These things have eternal consequences. The praises of thanksgiving from these families were overflowing to God.

I wondered if my troubles were temporary. Looking back, ten years of struggle, grief, loss and depression don't seem temporary to me. I guess when you have an eternal perspective, as God has and wants us to have, ten years is just a speck of time. I look forward to the time when these days will seem like they were temporary troubles.

At the memorial service, people said the oddest things:

"My son, Andrew, was born premature and we thought we'd lose him."

I wanted to point out that they didn't.

"Well, as least you can have more."

I wanted to yell, "I don't want more, I want the one who isn't here!"

"All things work together for those who love the Lord."

So are you saying I didn't love the Lord enough? What kind of comfort is that?

Another lady, who had her son a few days after we had Andrew, shared with me that they named their baby Andrew and asked if I would like to hold him. I know she was trying to offer me the comfort that she got from having her son in her arms, but I just couldn't do it. I thought I'd start crying and never stop. It took me years before I could hold a baby and then a few more to not be shocked at their warmth—my tactile memory of Andrew was of his coldness. A warm baby felt strange to my cold and empty arms.

I walked around aimlessly for months. Everything just seemed so futile. I was mad, angry and bewildered about what had happened. I wished things were different, but at the same time, I knew I couldn't change them. Each day the sun still rose and set, time marched by and the world went on. I knew that I should as well. However, it was hard.

Slowly my anger started to dissipate and I started remembering little joys we had with Andrew. He was such a beautiful baby, and I did get to nurse him a few times. We were lucky to see one or two smiles out of him. I even bathed him once, despite the wires and tubes protruding from his frail little body. In a few weeks, I noticed that I could go a few hours at a time without crying.

As my emotional strength returned, I started grappling with some of those hard questions lingering in my head. The first one was *how can I follow a God who allows babies to die?* This literally brought me to a crisis of faith; I had to decide what I believed and what I was going to do about it—why did I believe in God and if it was worth keeping the faith when bad things happen.

My faith was stripped down to nothing… I couldn't base it on what God was doing for me because I didn't like what he was doing. So why did I believe in God? Was it because I was raised in church? Maybe, but that is not a strong enough reason to choose God in a crisis. Was it because he called me to faith? Yes—God calls us and equips us through the

Holy Spirit. Was it because he always gives me good things? No, he hadn't always given me good things, but he did send us the best thing 2,000 years ago. Finally, I came to my conclusion; I love God because he sent his son Jesus to be a sacrifice for my sins so I might have a repaired relationship with him and live eternally with him in heaven. Isn't that enough?

God doesn't have to do more for me to love him because he already did it all. He provided the way to a relationship with him through Jesus. If I want the good things from God then I can't turn him away when the bad things happen. In fact, I decided that I can't even get through the bad things without him.

I need your light!

It was settled in my mind and heart; I wasn't turning away from God. However, I had nothing to say to him. It was hard to pray because of the anger and the tears, but I opened the Bible because of my newfound commitment. First, I turned to Psalm 119 because I love the poetry of the Psalms and 119 was the longest one. My eyes stopped at verse 130, "The unfolding of your words gives light; it gives understanding to the simple." *That's what I need,* I wrote in the margins, *understanding and light in my darkness.* I continued to seek comfort and understanding in God's word. I started reading the Psalms and praying them whenever they were relevant to me.

During October and November, I read forward from Psalm 119 until I hit Psalms 142 and 143. I lingered on these two pages of my Bible for three months. The words in these two Psalms were so poignant that I read them aloud to God daily—some days there were no other words to speak for a life that seemed so meaningless without my child.

> I cry to you, O Lord, I say, "You are my refuge my portion in the land of the living. Listen to my cry for I am in desperate need set me free from my prison that I may praise your name. Then the righteous will gather about me because of your goodness to me.

> O Lord, hear my prayer listen to my cries for mercy; In your faithful-ness and righteousness come to my relief. Do not bring your servant into judgment, for no one living is righteous before you. The enemy pursues me, he crushes me to the ground; he makes me dwell in darkness like those long dead. So my spirit grows faint within me; my heart within me is dismayed.

> I remember the days of long ago; I meditate on all your works and consider what your hands have done. I spread out my hands to you; my soul thirsts for you like a parched land.

Answer me quickly, O Lord, my spirit fails. Do not hide your face from me or I will be like those who go down to the pit Let the morning bring me word of your unfailing love, for I have put my trust in you. Show me the way I should go for to you I lift up my soul.   Psalm 142:8-143:8

Hear your child cry...

You are the light, I wrote in the margins. *Hear your child cry and bring me back into your light.* This was my only prayer for 93 days. The only words I could utter to God. These two pages of my Bible are tear-stained and worn because I daily read the words with passion and prayed for God's compassion.

God let me cry to him and grieve over Andrew for many months in the same way he let Elijah grieve after defeating the prophets of Baal in the Old Testament. God took care of me and fed me with choice morsels of his word in the same way he fed Elijah with bread from the ravens.

God was also often silent between those morsels of the word. I can compare this time in my life with a child who scrapes a knee and comes running to a parent for help. The parent will sit and hold the child, rocking him back and forth, until the screaming and crying subsides. The parent's words of comfort would be lost on the child in the midst of the tears; but when the tears subside, the parent speaks and the child is better. When my tears would subside, God would speak words of comfort and he helped me feel better.

Some of the words of comfort I marked in my margins over the next few months span the text of the Bible—some in the Old Testament, and some in the New. But they were always the words that God impressed upon me as I turned to him for help.

One day Brandon and I received the nicest note from Katherine, one of Andrew's NICU nurses in San Diego. She wrote Philippians 4:7-8: "And the peace of God, which transcends all understanding, will guard your heart in Christ Jesus." I marked this passage and the verses that followed in my Bible and added in the margin; *it's time to refocus and think on the good things of life*. Nurse Katherine also added in her note that she was praying that God would restore our joy. *Think on the good.*

We thought we would test God on this. We told him if someone was praying for our joy to be restored, then we would watch to see joy from him every day so we could have *something* to smile about. God was abundantly faithful to this request and did give us something to smile about every day, for a long time. Sometimes the dog would do something funny, like try to bring a four-foot palm frond through his one-foot wide dog door, or he would crawl up in my lap and lick the tears from my cheeks. Other times, God would send us joy in a phone call or letter or even directly through his word.

This search for daily joy gradually pulled us out of the crevasse we had fallen into in that valley of the shadow of death. We weren't out of the valley yet by any means, but we had recovered from the deepest pit in that valley.

Soon, after we prayed that God would show us joy each day, he led me to another passage that gave me a glimpse of what he was doing in my life.

> He gives strength to the weary and increases the power of the weak. Even youths grow tired and weary, and young men stumble and fall; but those who hope in the Lord will renew their strength. They will soar on wings like eagles; they will run and not grow weary, they will walk and not be faint. Isaiah 41:29-31

This is exactly what I needed next; I needed to remember that it was God who would give me the strength to walk and not be faint. My emotional burden, grief and depression would weigh me down so heavily I thought I would never be able to stand up under it. I was trying to do the right things like exercise and take care of myself, but most days if I was out walking the dog or jogging, I would nearly fall over with the weight of my grief. My thoughts would always come around to the fact that there I was, trying to get rid of pregnancy weight, and I had nothing to show for it! It was maddening.

This verse gave me hope. I had indeed grown weary. I was stumbling and falling from the weight of my grief, but I also deliberately put my hope in God to get me through my dark valley and he had given me a way. I didn't need to run or soar, I was just happy that God would help me walk and not be faint. I marked in the margin of my Bible: *God is my strength to keep me walking forward in my grief.*

God will help me walk

We were entering the holiday season—it would have been Andrew's first Christmas and it didn't feel very joyous to us. In fact, I could not even decorate that year. My friends used to tease me about being "Martha Stewart." I would decorate for every season—especially Christmas. I decorated every room in the house for Christmas. I loved how it made a home feel festive and joyous. The year Andrew died changed that. I could not feel joy when so much of me hurt. All I could do was hang a few ornaments from ribbons in the window.

I usually looked forward to Christmas from the time Thanksgiving hit. I threw fun wrapping parties and cookie exchanges and took every opportunity to share the hospitality of the season. This year I had to force myself through it.

I decided to continue my much-anticipated wrapping party and scheduled it early in December, hoping that the routine and activity of being festive would help me celebrate the season. Twelve ladies came and sat in a circle on the floor laughing, sharing stories and wrapping Christmas gifts. I sat numbly on the couch watching them as if I were dreaming. I could not connect with any of them because for the first time in my life, I was dreading Christmas.

65

All of the plans my friends and I had made earlier that summer had been dashed to pieces when Andrew died. Not only was I still grieving over my son, but now I also had the added grief of the dreams and plans we had for our family.

Brandon and I decided it would be best to get out of the house for Christmas so we took a hop over to the big island of Hawaii and stayed at the military camp by the Volcano National Park. The cabins were quaint with a bedroom, living room and mini kitchen. The living room was adorned with a large rock fireplace which looked very out of place in the tropical climate. On Christmas Eve, we found out why the cabin had a fireplace. A storm had brought cold rain to the mountain top retreat and strong winds had knocked out the power. Brandon and I were happy to have a reason to light the fire and forget that it was Christmas Eve.

We ate crackers with cheese and salami and enjoyed the comfort of the warm fire on that blustery evening. This was a much-needed getaway to help us get through a rough time while we were so far away from family. The lack of phone, television and computers let us take a break from the world and rest.

During that Christmas season, God showed me another comforting message during one of our sessions together. This time it was as if he was saying, "I know what you are going through. I've been there too. You are going to be okay."

I got this from Hebrews 5:7-10:

During the days of Jesus' life on earth, he
offered up prayers and petitions with loud
cries and tears to the one who could save
him from death, and he was heard because
of his reverent submission.

Wow! I wrote in the margin next to this verse, *Jesus knows grief!*
Jesus cried out to God with loud cries and tears! He knows
grief. Indeed. He knows grief on many levels.

Because of the focus of Jesus coming as a baby at
Christmas time, it gave me the opportunity to ponder the
sacrifices made by both Jesus and God the Father.
Jesus knew grief because he lived as man on this earth.
He lost his friend Lazarus, he grieved over Jerusalem,
and he offered his holy self up for a final sacrifice for
our sins—separating himself from his Father for a time.
He knows what it's like to lose a loved one, and he knows
what it's like to be alone and afraid. If anyone knows grief
it's Jesus.

Of all the cards, notes and letters we received when
Andrew died, the words that were shared by someone who
had lost a child were always the most meaningful and
comforting. It was important to me that someone took the
time to revisit the grief to share with me the fact that I, too,
would survive. Jesus' words had the same effect on me. He
knew what I was going through and he could comfort me
better than anyone could.

As far as losing a son, God could be empathet-
ic about that one, too. God lost Jesus for a time; he lost

his son's physical presence next to him in the Heavenly realms when Jesus laid aside his glory and came to Earth. He also lost Jesus for a time on the cross when Jesus was taking the punishment for our sins. God's own son was killed—for me. God would certainly know how to comfort me in my grief.

This revelation gave me the security that God could expertly walk me through this valley I was in. I trusted that I could hope in him because he was revealing himself to me.

God's last message to me for that calendar year in the pages of my Bible was from 1 Peter:

> And the God of all grace, who called you to his eternal glory in Christ; after you have suffered for a little while, will himself restore you and make you strong, firm and steadfast. I Peter 5:10

God always re- stores

The note in the margin of my Bible on that page was my hope and prayer for the New Year: *God always has restoration at the end of a trial. Thank you for restoring me from my initial grief over Andrew!*

I hoped the New Year would bring that restoration in the form of other children who would answer the longing in my heart. I really came far in the three months since Andrew died; I could make it most of the day without falling apart and soon I could go for a whole week without shedding tears. My restoration was in the works, and as long as I looked to God for the answers, he was faithful to provide them.

I still was sad and wanted to hold and raise my son. I wished I could have heard him laugh and talk. I never saw him take his first steps or celebrate his birthday. He never got to sleep in his crib or play with his toys. I grieve over those lost dreams, even to this day. I know I cannot bring my son back; I can only press on knowing some day, I too will walk with God. Then Andrew can show me around the streets of heaven.

God allows us to grieve for a time so we will turn to him with our hard questions. Grieving is an important process for getting past the pain. Sometimes grief can come to us over different circumstances than a child's death.

You could be grieving over an illness, a prodigal, the loss of a job, a move, a dream deferred, or change of any kind. Many things in this life can cause upset. The important thing is to allow yourself some time to grieve over it so you can accept it. You don't need to pretend that everything is okay. You don't need to put on a smiling mask at church. You don't have to be happy all the time because you are a Christian. Life is hard and there are many twists and turns that we don't expect. I think God wants us to acknowledge our pain, but instead of bathing in it, I think he wants us to bring it to him; that's what I did. For many months, I brought my doubts, fear, frustrations and anger right to God's feet. You'll be amazed at what he did with them.

Chapter Four
Crying out to God

I loathe my very life; therefore I will give free reign to my complaint and speak out in the bitterness of my soul. Job 10:1

I poured out my complaints to God because I wanted to understand *why.* Why did I lose one of my tubes and my first-born son? Why was I now having so many miscarriages? I was desperate to understand these circumstances in context of what I knew about God. It took many years to finally understand some of the answers God was giving me; it was a journey marked by mountains of prayer and understanding, and valleys of darkness, doubt and depression. It was a journey that I would not have taken given the choice—but it's one I'm glad to have experienced if only because it has deepened my faith and helped me know God in new ways.

Still, during those days in the valley of the shadow of death, I was plagued with seemingly unanswerable questions in the midst of my circumstances: If God is the author of life, why was there so much death in mine? If he really loved me, why was I in so much pain? Moreover, if children are a blessing from God, why was I losing mine?

"It's just not fair," I told a friend one day as we sat in her kitchen drinking tea. "I have been faithful, I don't think I took God for granted, I prayed every day and look where all that got me. I've almost died, I've lost my son and I can't seem to hold on to a pregnancy. I haven't lost faith in God for my salvation, but I can't go around boasting in him. I'm just going to be a 'quiet Christian' from now on. I'll go to church, I'll say grace, but that's it. There's no reason to be 'on fire' for God if he's going to keep making my life hard."

My friends, who had been so dear and important to me while I grappled with the immediate grief of Andrew's death, continued their encouragement with well-meaning phrases like, "I'm sure God will bless you after what you've been through." I started hearing that as, "God sure owes you a blessing now!" I heard it so much, I started to believe it.

God owes me!

Surely, God owes me a blessing, I thought. *After all, I've been through so much! I've still been faithful even though I don't understand. I have not complained. I've suffered more loss and pain than anyone I know! I am worthy of a blessing because I've hurt so much!*

I took it to God, and he came back at me almost immediately with a difficult answer. Actually, I didn't *ask* the question. Like Jeopardy™, I gave him the answer, "YOU OWE ME!" He replied with a question that was hard to take, but necessary for my journey of healing and growth. In essence, he asked, "Who are you to say what I owe you?"

I opened my Bible one quiet day in February, arrogantly thinking, "S*how me that blessing you owe me!*" I turned to Luke chapter 17.

> "Suppose one of you had a servant plowing or looking after the sheep. Would he say to the servant when he comes in from the field, 'Come along now and sit down to eat'? Would he not rather say, 'Prepare my supper, get yourself ready and wait on me while I eat and drink, after that you may eat and drink'? Would he thank the servant because he did what he was told to do? So you, also, when you have done everything you were told to do, should say, 'We are unworthy servants; we have only done our duty,'" Luke 17:7-10.

Show me a blessing

Ouch! reads the note in the margin. *God doesn't have to thank me for doing what he's asked me to do. He does not owe me any blessing!* I stood convicted. I cried as I looked on those words. How prideful I'd become! When

Ouch! did I put myself in the center? When did I remove God and replace his authority with my own?

If I call myself a disciple of Jesus, then he has purchased me by faith as a bondservant. The original Greek translates servant as slave—a term we're uncomfortable with today, but an accurate illustration. A slave does the job determined by the master; that's his duty. He doesn't do it because he gets a blessing from the master. He does the job because the master has requested it.

It's hard to relate to having or being a slave, but most of us have at least held a job. We go to that job and do the work assigned, and while we would love for our boss to say, "You've worked so hard, take a day off!" The reality is he won't. We've done what he's paid us to do.

Being a wife and/or mother is also a good modern-day example; we do the chores and take care of the children and the house because it's what we do. We may have help or we may not, but we still do the work. Our children don't spend the day thanking us for our work—but we do it anyway. When our spouse comes home, he doesn't say (as much as we'd like him to), "Darling! You've done the dishes, made the beds, done the laundry and cleaned the house! What a great job! Sit! I'll pour you some lemonade. I'll make dinner and you just relax!" No, he more likely says, "Boy was my day rough. What's for dinner? When's it ready?" And that's okay. It's our job to do our work whether anyone notices or says thank you.

So it is with God. He is not obliged to me; nothing is owed me on my merit and good works, or for my trials.

He doesn't have to say, "Oh, you handled that trial so well! You are such a good servant. Since you did that for me, let me serve you a banquet. You sit down, I'll clean up!" It's not about what God will do for me, but instead it's about me not being able to repay what he already did for me— his sacrifice on the cross given freely, but at great cost.

My Master has told this servant to walk through trials and I have. I've endured them—not for a blessing or praise and glory, but to be made more like Christ. No doubt, he is proud of my strength. I could even hope that he's marked it down somewhere for a time when our lives are judged in the refiner's fire; but there is no party in heaven because I've endured it. Through my trials, my attitude ought to be that of the servant, "I have only done what I've been told," because I can do no more and I should do no less.

Although this message is hard to swallow—that we are but servants of the Lord—it is not the whole story. We are also his children (1 John 3:1, "How great is the love the Father has lavished on us, that we should be called children of God! And that is what we are!"), and his friends (John 15:14, "You are my friends if you do what I command."). Nonetheless, I have learned that it's prudent to remember I've been bought with a price and I am ultimately called to do his will in this world.

The thing about God's correction is this: He is not a harsh being who sits up in heaven waiting for us to mess up so he can rebuke us. He is really a loving parent, and like our earthly parents, makes sure we feel His love after a correction. When I asked, "WHY ARE YOU DOING THIS TO ME?" he took me to the book of Job, a classic tale of loss and grief. "Blessed is the man whom God corrects; so do not despise the discipline of the Almighty." Job 5:17 says.

"*Bad things are not from the Lord,*" I wrote in the margin of my Bible, "*but he allows them sometimes to mold us and shape us more like Him—that is the blessing He gives.*"

Bad things are not from God

In comparison with this thought, I referenced James 1:17, "Every good and perfect gift is from above, coming down from the Father of the heavenly lights, who does not change like shifting shadows."

God was showing me that occasionally, bad things happen but he can use the trouble in life to give us the good and perfect gifts he desires for us. The biggest thing he desires is our growth; our ability to use the trouble and grief to lean on him, to learn his character and ultimately to be conformed into his image of us.

I pondered God's loving answer—*I want you to grow in me*—in contrast to my demands for answers and blessings as I continued to read the book of James.

I stopped near the end in chapter five which, in my Bible, is subtitled *Patience in Suffering.* "*That's for me,*" I thought. "*I'm sure this is how God wants me to behave in my trials.*" Verses 10-12 confirmed that:

"Brothers, as an example of patience in the face of suffering, take the prophets who spoke in the name of the Lord. As you know, we consider blessed those who have persevered. You have heard of Job's perseverance and have seen what the Lord finally brought about. The Lord is full of compassion and mercy." James 5:10-12

Wait on the Lord

Those who persevered are blessed...wait for God's timing and his blessing will come. When I continue to walk this path laid before me, he may bless me as I persevere in faith. The Lord indeed blessed Job, but not right away. God wants to bless us because he is full of compassion and mercy towards us. Like his salvation, his blessings are an overflow of his mercy and compassion on his children. Like an earthly father, he does not really like it when I demand something from him as if I am the one in charge.

The next time I queried God, I was not as demanding, even though there were some hard questions that I really wanted answered. God didn't always respond to me as notably as he did when I demanded blessings, but I continued to bring my questions to him. After all, I was trying to establish a relationship with him. When there is something wrong in any of my other relationships, we talk about it—so it made sense to continue pursuing answers.

"God, why wouldn't you heal Andrew?" I asked him one day. "After all, Jesus healed everyone who asked him." I echoed the words of Jeremiah in 20:18 both in my prayers and in my journals; "Why did I ever come out of the womb to see trouble and sorrow and to end my days in shame?" *Many days I have felt this way—like it would just be easier to die* say the notes in the margin.

God was silent on that one for a long time. The only time he gave me any kind of clue was when one day in church I read, "…but this happened that the work of God may be displayed." (John 9:3). The disciples were asking Jesus why a certain man was born blind. They wondered if it was because of his sin or the sin of his parents'. Jesus answered that the man was born blind, not because of sin, but to show God's glory when Jesus healed him. This gave me hope that Andrew's death was not because we had sinned or because we didn't have enough faith for him to be healed. God had a plan. I had to learn to trust it.

As I was learning to trust God's judgment while dealing with my infertility, there were stories in the media about teenage girls having babies and trying to flush them down the toilet or leave them in the trash can. That was enough to send me over the edge. How unfair! Didn't those stupid girls know there are thousands of women out there who are heartbroken over not having children? What a stab in the heart to hear about babies dying in trash cans when our arms are empty and aching! Then, as if to pour lemon juice on the wound, the media began reporting mothers who were drowning and strangling their children.

"God," I boldly said one night after turning off the news, "this is not fair! Why do people who don't take care of their kids still get them?" During the next week and a half, I ran across three scripture verses that even today remain engraved on my heart. The first was Psalm 73; I encourage you to read the whole Psalm if you are wondering why the wicked seem to prosper while the righteous suffer. Verses 16-17 summed it up for me. "When I tried to understand all this, it was oppressive to me till I entered the sanctuary of God; then I understood their final destiny." The note in the margin reads, *don't let the prosperity of the wicked take your eyes off Jesus—they will have to answer to him one day.*

God also showed me Proverbs 23:17-18; "Do not let your heart envy sinners, but always be zealous for the fear of the Lord. There is surely a future hope for you and your hope will not be cut off." The note in the margin by this verse was what I knew God was saying to me; *Don't want what others have—be concerned with what I ask you do to.* Wow! That was direct. God wanted me to be concerned with my obedience to him, not about what others were doing regardless of their wickedness. I needed to keep my eyes on my own plate; it was full enough.

Don't want what others have

Full enough, indeed. I continued on the roller coaster of mountaintop faith and dark, depressive valleys and my husband, friends and family felt helpless. That's the thing about faith struggles—they can only be worked out between you and God. People can quote verses or sit and cry with you, but in the end, it's just you and God who have to wrestle it out. That's why it is so important to talk with him. He's big enough to handle the hard questions. I'm sure that by now there is nothing he hasn't heard, and certainly nothing that would surprise him.

For months, I vacillated between praising God for

his love and doubting he cared at all. If you looked at my journals, you would think I was bipolar (with no offense to those who suffer from this debilitating disease). The extreme highs and lows sometimes even alarmed me. One day I would be full of energy and the next it was all I could do to get out of bed.

The margins of my Bible became saturated with notes, prayers and questions for God. I heard him speak to me so loudly just months earlier, and now I wondered if he was even there. When I cried out to him, I got silence in return, so I poured through the Psalms taking a morbid comfort in the pain and emotion expressed by David and the other Psalmists. Psalm 13:1-4 is underlined and highlighted;

"How long, O Lord? Will you forget me forever? How long will you hide your face from me? How long must I wrestle with my thoughts and every day have sorrow in my heart? How long will my enemy triumph over me? Look on answer, O Lord, and me my God. Give light to my eyes, or I will sleep in death; my enemy will say, 'I have overcome him,' and my foes will rejoice when I fall."

I moved on to Psalm 22, marking verses 9-11, 14 and 15;

"Yet you brought me out of the womb; you made me trust in you even at my mother's breast. From birth I was cast upon you; from my mother's womb you have been my God. Do not be far from me, for trouble is near and there is no one to help...I am poured out like water, and all my bones are out of joint. My heart has turned to wax; it has melted away within me. My strength is dried up like a potsherd, and my tongue sticks to the roof of my mouth; you lay me in the dust of the earth."

Lord, I have no strength left to fight, I wrote in the margin. Still nothing from God. I pleaded Psalm 27:7-9 before God;

"Hear my voice when I call, O Lord; be merciful to me and answer me. My heart says of you, "Seek his face!" Your face, Lord, I will seek. Do not hide your face from me..." *So why do I feel like he has?*

Then I read verses 13-14 of that Psalm:

"I am still confident of this: I will see the goodness of the Lord in the land of the living. Wait for the Lord; be strong and take heart and wait for the Lord."

I'm tired of waiting! I noted in the margin. There was still so much pain in my heart.

I'm tired of waiting

To make matters more complex, Brandon and I were still trying to get pregnant. Every month was emotional mayhem hoping, praying and even begging for a pregnancy, and extreme disappointment when it didn't happen. Or worse, I would test positive for pregnancy only to find out I was having a miscarriage. I cried out to God, pleading for him to hear me. Help me. Heal me. I prayed the beginning of Psalm 28;

> "To you I call, O Lord my Rock; do not turn a deaf ear to me. For if you remain silent, I will be like those who have gone down to the pit. Hear my cry for mercy as I call to you for help, as I lift up my hands towards your Most Holy Place."

I prayed Psalm 43:3-4 as another attempt to reach God through this silence.

> "Send forth your light and your truth, let them guide me; let them bring me to your holy mountain, to the place where you dwell. Then will I go to the altar of God, to God, my joy and my delight. I will praise you with the heart O God, my God."

The prayers penned in my journals echo my desire for God to hear and heal me. *I lift up to you this feeling in the back of my mind that I am pregnant. If I am, I beg you to remove the fear and help me trust in you. Lord, I am holding on to you, I know you are capable to let this child in me live.* And a few days later; *I feel like I'm having another miscarriage. Please keep me from falling into depression, again.* From my perspective, my prayers were going unanswered and I was losing faith.

Each month when I found out I was pregnant, I struggled with whether or not to tell Brandon—he would get so worried about me. I fell into a pattern of waiting until the miscarriage to tell him. I carried the burden and the fear myself; I felt so alone.

"Record my lament; list my tears on your scroll—are they not in your record?" (Psalm 56:8). *Don't you know how much I'm hurting, Lord?*

Months passed and I wept over Psalm 77;

> I cried out to God for help; I cried out to God to hear me. When I was in distress, I sought the Lord; at night I stretched out untiring hands and my soul refused to be comforted. I remembered you, O God, and I groaned; I mused, and my spirit grew faint. You kept my eyes from closing; I was too troubled to speak.

Do you know how much I'm hurting?

83

I thought about the former days, the years of long ago; I remembered my songs in the night. My heart mused and my spirit inquired: Will the Lord reject forever? Will he never show his favor again? Has his unfailing love vanished forever? Has his promise failed for all time? Has God forgotten to be merciful? Has he in anger withheld his compassion?

Don't you know how much I'm hurting, Lord?

Then I thought, "To this I will appeal: the years of the right hand of the Most High." I will remember the deeds of the Lord; yes, I will remember your miracles of long ago. I will meditate on all your works and consider all your mighty deeds.

Your ways, O God, are holy. What God is so great as our God? You are the God who performs miracles; you display your power among the peoples. With your might arm you redeemed your people the descendants of Jacob and Joseph.

Where are you when I'm hurting? Why don't I see your miracles and your power? Why do I still hurt so much? Why is there still so much death and pain in my life? If you really love me, God, why do I hurt so badly?

I couldn't see it then, but I had succumbed to the oldest trick in the book: Doubt.

Where are you, God?

Chapter Five
When the Devil Came for Tea

hen the Lord God said to the woman, "What is this you have done?" The woman said, "The serpent deceived me, and I ate." Genesis 3:13

I was tired of my circumstances and of praying to a God who I thought didn't hear me, so I closed my Bible and went to see who kept pounding at the door in my mind. It was the devil, spewing lies and instilling doubt in my life. I invited him in for tea, and we talked about all my loss; a tubal pregnancy that nearly killed me... my ruptured appendix that again nearly killed me...our son Andrew who was born with a heart defect and lived two weeks...and now miscarriages. He stayed for a long time convincing me that God must not love me. My Bible gathered dust in the corner as I entertained these lies of the devil and continued having miscarriages.

The Bible says that God gives children to those he loves, the devil taunted me in my mind. *He must not love you because he keeps giving you children and taking them away from you.*

Sarah was barren, so was Rachel. Elizabeth, the mother of John the Baptist, was barren most all her life. When those women prayed for children, God answered their prayers. He doesn't answer yours. Wonder if that means he doesn't really love you?

I embraced these lies from the devil and took a trip back into the lonely darkness in the bottom of the pit I was trying so hard to escape. *That's right. God keeps taking children away from me. How is it that the author of life would create in me something that couldn't live?* I started to think God was taunting me with pregnancies and miscarriages every few months; as if he were saying, "Here, you can have a child...just kidding!" With each consecutive miscarriage, my doubt grew as if it were a new child growing inside me. I started living in the garbage dump strewn around me by the devil, thinking it must be God's will for me to accept a crappy life.

Now I know that when we accept the garbage of life as God's will for us, then the devil has done his job. He is crafty and wise to the ways of man. Our failures are his specialty and when he can get one of his dark, poisonous talons in us, he will not let go until his foothold becomes our stronghold. My doubt in God's love for me became the driving force behind all my thoughts. I let the devil instill disbelief and steal my hope. I had nothing left. I was living in a pit of selfishness, with a growing worldly view and a diminishing spirit. Life without hope, I've learned, is dismal.

King Solomon was right when he wrote in Ecclesiastes that there is nothing new under the sun; for the Bible even addresses what happens to the person whose hope has been lost. Proverbs 13:12 says that hope deferred makes the heart sick. Hope is the desire of some good, but it is stronger than a wish because hope is instilled by *evidence* of good. We have hope because we have seen that good is possible. At this point, however, any evidence of existing good in my life had faded and was expertly hidden by the darkness surrounding me. I could not see God, so I had no evidence of hope. The only evidence I had was of loss and doubt. This was deceptive, circumstantial evidence.

Worse than being duped by the devil, I became a classic hypocrite. I went to church, led the Women's Ministry and taught Bible studies all while living in the garbage pit the devil designed and decorated just for me.

Aloud I worshipped God on Sundays, but inwardly I was wasting away in despair. I helped women understand their worth in God's eyes, but never believed that those same words applied to me. Instead of turning to God, I hid in my darkness.

Job's friend, Bildad the Shumite, in his response to Job's lamentations of his loss, said this of the person who has lost all hope:

> "Can papyrus grow tall where there is no
>   marsh?
> Can reeds thrive without water?
> While still growing and uncut,
>   they wither more quickly than
>   grass.
> Such is the destiny of all who forget God:
>   so perishes the hope of the
>   godless.
> What he trusts in is fragile;
>   what he relies on is a spider's
>   web.
> He leans on his web, but it gives way;
>   he clings to it, but it does not
>   hold." (Job 8:11-15)

This was my life. It was crumbling around me. I was depressed and withdrawn. I could barely get out of bed each day and when I did, I usually only made it as far as the couch. I relied on the television and reruns of *Little House on the Prairie* to fill my life. But I was still empty. I was still mad. And I felt all alone.

We moved to Texas from Hawaii the summer after Andrew died. Although Hawaii was a beautiful place to live, I was grateful to move away from the sadness permeating our lives there.

When we arrived in San Antonio, we fought a new battle with our situation: *How do we answer the question, "Do you have kids?"* Whenever we met new friends in our neighborhood or church, that dreaded question would always surface; "Do you have any kids?" This seemingly kind, even polite inquiry ripped open the wounds in my spirit and my emotions. *Do we have kids? Well yes, we've had a few kids—but we weren't allowed to keep them.* Do I answer this question forthright? *Yes, but they are dead.* Talk about a conversation stopper! I settled on the answer, "Not right now" because it was honest without being awkward. Next people would invariably say, "Oh, you're young—there's still time," or, "There is always adoption." They thought they were helping me, but on inside I was screaming as these words ripped my heart to shreds. If they kept pressing the issue, I would eventually retort with a sour, "I've had kids, but they died."

Brandon and I spent our time just trying to survive. I tried to distract myself with a home business and Brandon traveled a lot with his job. Often, Brandon would come home from work to find me lying on the couch, lifeless and uninterested. He did his best to help me; we went out to dinner on those nights so we could distract ourselves from the darkness surrounding us.

I frequently had angry outbursts that actually scared me. I threw tantrums over not being able to open a jar of spaghetti sauce, or if something didn't go as I'd planned. It was as if I was two different beings—one watching this behavior from afar and not being able to stop it, and another in the midst of the behavior lashing out at anything I could.

One day I was weeding a flower patch in the back yard of our rented home. It was right after lunch and very hot. I took a break to get some ice-cold water from the kitchen and discovered I was locked out of the house. The latch on the sliding door had somehow engaged when I first went outside. I tried to get around to the front of the house through the side fence only to realize it was locked from the outside. It wouldn't have helped anyway because the front door was always locked and the garage door was shut. I went into a rage hitting the fence, kicking the house, roughing up the sliding glass door and screaming profanities that are quite out of character for me. For almost an hour, I threw a bigger temper tantrum than a three-year-old in a candy store. All the time, I watched myself carry on, knowing this was not right, but not being able to stop myself. Exhausted, I finally laid down on the grass in the shade and cried myself to sleep. I was thankful when Brandon came home early that day to rescue me. He chuckled at the images when he heard my story which helped put it in perspective for me.

This dreary existence finally shattered one weekend in November when it was apparent that I was enduring my fifth miscarriage. I confirmed my pregnancy two weeks before Brandon left for a four-month deployment to Bosnia. Two days before he left, I started bleeding and we both felt that familiar and deplorable wave of frustration and grief.

Brandon left for Europe on a Saturday and by Sunday, I was still cramping but had not officially miscarried, so as my habit was, I went to church.

Our church celebrated communion four times a year—and this Sunday happened to be one of those days. I sat in the back row and cried through the whole service. Our small congregation mistakenly thought I was distraught over Brandon's departure. I was really crying because I was fed up with my life. I was mad at God and I knew I couldn't take communion. One thing I know about God was that he doesn't take our commitments to him lightly. I knew that by taking communion, I was professing my faith in him and that doing so on this day would be a lie. I didn't trust God anymore. It seemed like he had taken so much from me!

Before the communion plate came to me, I escaped my pew and slid out the back door. I could barely see to drive home for the torrent of tears streaming from my eyes. By the time I arrived home, I was crying so hard I could hardly breathe. I threw myself on the couch and cursed *You* everything; God for hating me, Brandon for leaving me, *are the* and myself for not being able to have children. *author*
of life

Then a distantly familiar and quiet voice stirred *and* deep within my soul. "It's not me you should be mad at." *you* *What?* *took*
my
"It's not me with whom you should be mad." *babies*

Is that you, God? What do you mean its not you— away you are the author of life. You have the power to give life *from* *and take it away, and you keep taking it away from me.* *me!*

93

Then as if in a dream, I stirred to retrieve my Bible from its dusty corner. My insides were on fire, and moving against the paralyzing darkness in my pit, I slowly opened my old friend whom I had abandoned in the past months. Its weight on my lap felt oddly comfortable, and the crinkle of the pages as I turned them warmed an outer layer of ice that formed around my heart. I opened to the bookmark I left the last time I read; Job 9:17-27:

We misunderstand God because we can't see...

God wants what is best for me!

He would crush me with a storm and multiply my wounds for no reason. He would not let me regain my breath but will overwhelm me with misery. If it is a matter of justice, who will summon him? Even if I were innocent, my mouth would condemn me; if I were blameless, it would pronounce me guilty. Although I am blameless I have no concern for myself; I despise my own life. It is all the same; that is why I say, 'He destroys both the blameless and the wicked.' When a scourge brings sudden death, he mocks the despair of the innocent. When a land falls into the hands of the wicked, he blindfolds its judges. If it is not he, then who is it? My days are swifter than a runner, they fly away without a glimpse of joy. They skim past like boats of papyrus, like eagles swooping down on their prey. If I say, 'I will forget

my complaint, I will change my expression
and smile,' I still dread all my sufferings,
for I know you will not hold me innocent.

Notes spatter the margins of the two pages that were lying open on my lap: *Sometimes we misunderstand God because we can't see what he does…it's a circle of our perception… We think it's bad because we can't see it from God's eyes…God wants what is best for me!*

I was being torn apart in a spiritual tug-of-war; demons and angels surrounded me, fighting for my attention. *See, he would crush you with storms and multiply your wounds for no reason; he will overwhelm you with misery, he mocks the despair of the innocent!* spit the demons. *Look at the end,* countered the angels. *Your days are swift and you need to restore this relationship. Look at your notes—you can't see God's perspective. He wants what's best for you.*

I needed to hear more so I turned the pages until I stared at the beginning of the book of Haggai, a prophet who wrote God's word after the Israelites were released from Babylonian captivity. The chapter is only 38 verses long, but the message packed a punch and woke me up from my dismal stupor.

I could feel God encouraging me, calling me out of captivity. I read the words through teary eyes. Tears fell off my face making water spots that wrinkled circles into the pages. I underlined verses as God impressed them on my heart. "Is it a time for you yourselves to be living in

your paneled houses, while (the temple) remains a ruin?"
(1:4). New Testament verses about our bodies being the
temple of the Holy Spirit came to mind. I was neglecting
the temple because my relationship with God was in ruins.
I read on:

"Now this is what the Lord
Almighty says, 'Give careful thought to
your ways. You have planted much, but
have harvested little' (1:5);

'Give careful thought to your ways. Go
up into the mountains and bring down
timber and build the house, so that I may
take pleasure in it and be honored,' says
the Lord.

'You expected much, but see, it turned out
to be little. What you brought home, I blew
away. Why?' declares the Lord Almighty.
'Because of my house, which remains a
ruin, while each of you is busy with his
own house. Therefore, because of you the
heavens have withheld their dew and the
earth its crops.

I called for a drought on the fields and the
mountains, on the grain, the new wine, the
oil and whatever the ground produces, on

men and cattle, and on the labor of your hands.'" (1:8-11)

I was neglecting God's work, putting my will before his and it was drying me up. There was drought in my life because I refused to let God fill me.

"'Be strong, all you people of the land,' declares the Lord, 'and work. For I am with you,' declares the Lord Almighty. 'This is what I covenanted with you when you came out of Egypt. And my Spirit remains among you. Do not fear...' (2:4-5)

'The glory of this present house will be greater than the glory of the former house,' says the Lord Almighty. 'And in this place I will grant peace,' declares the Lord Almighty" (2:9).

A light came on in my darkness. That light, which started as a small flame, was igniting into a bonfire, burning up my doubt and anger and chasing away the deceitful guest who came for tea but moved in. I considered what I read and I realized I needed to repair the temple within. My relationship with God was in ruins because I let doubt, circumstances and selfish perspectives rule my emotions. I was mad at God about my miscarriages and fertility problems because I thought they were his fault.

"Consider your ways," said the Lord; God was showing me that these problems are of the world because there is sin and death where we live. It dawned on me that it wasn't God's fault at all. It was because of the devil, the enemy I had befriended, that I was experiencing so much loss and misery in my life. It wasn't God's best for me, but it was what the world has come to.

This temple is more glorious than the one torn down!

God has grant-ed it peace!

"God, I'm sorry for blaming you," I wept aloud. As soon as I uttered those words, a ball of warmth landed on my head and covered my body like syrup on a stack of pancakes. The heat of God's love filled my body; peace and forgiveness flooded my soul. I wrote in the pages of my Bible, "*This temple is now more glorious than the one torn down, and God has granted it peace!*"

I was caught up in a moment of worship and put my favorite worship tape into the stereo. I stood with my arms raised and my eyes closed when I saw a lovely, glorious, glowing figure of Jesus reaching his arms toward me. I was touched and healed from my miscarriage at that very moment. No bleeding, no cramping, no miscarriage. Just healing; physically, spiritually and emotionally. Totally. Completely.

The end of the notes on that page in my Bible reads, "*I feel the love, peace and joy from God like I have never before known. Praise God, the giver of life and peace!*" Now the tears flowing down my face were tears of joy and relief.

C.S. Lewis wrote in *Till We Have Faces,* "I know now, Lord, why you utter no answer. You yourself are the answer. Before your face, questions die away. What other word would suffice?"

God doesn't leave us when we are downtrodden. We usually leave him because we can't understand, in our limited perceptions, what he intends to accomplish through our trials. See for yourself—the Bible is filled with God telling us, "I am with you." Jesus, who is called Emmanuel, meaning God with us, was sent to us so we might dwell with God forever. Now on Earth, and forevermore. God has not abandoned you. He is simply waiting. Waiting for you to call to him again—just like in the poem I wrote a few years ago:

Through the Clouds

Days and days of cloudy skies

Cold

Gloom

Consuming grief

Where are you, God?

Do you not hear my cries?

Are you there?

I long for a glimpse of your faithfulness

some hope

as I endure this darkness

Then, a break in the clouds

A beam of sunlight

draws toward my face

radiating His love
Gently kissing
my tear-stained cheek
Reminding me
He was there all the time
Behind the clouds
Watching
Waiting
for me to call

Now that I have the benefit of hindsight, knowing that God is patiently waiting for us to come back to him during our time of trial, let me share some things the perspective of time has shown me.

I recently attended my 20th high school reunion where I learned something very interesting about myself. My high school friends recalled fun stories involving me and I swear I didn't remember those events; the trials I have been writing about caused me to forget everything good in my life. I became so used to having a hard life that I forgot life could ever be so easy or happy. I let the trauma I had been through define me in a dark way that washed out any joy or happiness I had known in the past.

I believe this is why the fourth chapter of Philippians is dedicated to resolving issues by thinking on the good.

"Finally, brothers, whatever is true, whatever is noble, whatever is right,

> whatever is pure, whatever is lovely,
> whatever is admirable—if anything is
> excellent or praiseworthy—think about
> such things. Whatever you have learned or
> received or hear from me, or seen in me—
> put it into practice. And the God of peace
> will be with you." Philippians 4:8-9.

This is a good lesson and something to put into practice—so I did. Each week for the past few years, I've taken time to reflect on the good of that week. I write down what I have accomplished, the fun times we had and those events that have made me feel blessed. This activity helps me realize that even when a week is filled with challenges like my husband deploying to Iraq or problems with my computer, there is also good to balance out the challenge.

Trials in our lives also cause us to forget God. As evidenced by my behavior during my miscarriages, I forgot all that God is able to do. I forgot his lordship over my life, his love, his compassion and his mercy. I forgot his abilities and his character. As a result, I grew empty. I had no purpose. I had lost all hope. This must have been how David felt when he penned Psalm 42.

> As the deer pants for streams of water, so
> my soul pants for you, O God. My soul
> thirsts for God, for the living God. When
> can I go and meet with God? My tears
> have been my food day and night, while

I feel so empty without God...I used to be so close to him...

Re-member him and he will help you make a new connec-tion

men say to me all day long, "Where is your God?" These things I remember as I pour out my soul: How I used to go with the multitude, leading the procession to the house of God, with shouts of joy and thanksgiving among a festive throng. Why are you so downcast, O my soul? Why so disturbed within me? Put your hope in God, for I will yet praise him, my savior and my God. My soul is downcast within me; therefore I will remember you from the land of the Jordan, the heights of Hermon—from mount Mizar. (Psalm 42:1-6)

I marked in the margin of my Bible, *I feel so empty without God...I feel so far away. I used to be so close to him...* and as if God was answering my lament, there is another note directly underneath: *Remember him and he will help you make a new connection.*

Part of my new connection with God was in Psalm 25:15-18 which reads,

"My eyes are ever on the Lord, for only he will release my feet from the snare. Turn to me and be gracious to me, for I am lonely and afflicted. The troubles of my heart have multiplied; free me from my anguish. Look upon my affliction and my distress and take away all my sins."

This was the cry of my soul when I saw how far away I had drifted from the only one who was able to keep me afloat.

I've learned something else about women in trials while looking back over these years in my life: women love to stuff emotions. I see it all the time, especially in marriages, when the wife will be angry or upset, yet she will not voice it. She will mope around or briskly clean the house, but when her husband asks, "What's wrong?" he is supplied with a curt, *"Nothing."* There are many issues I have with this scenario, but I'm using it here to point out an obvious fact: Women tend to stuff their emotions. We think we are being stupid for feeling the way we do, or sometimes we're just tired of crying so we put an end to it. That is what I did.

One day, I was so tired of crying all the time that I just decided to stop. I turned off the nozzle to the tears and told myself, "That's enough!" It worked for a while. At least I thought it did.

The reality is that we cannot just turn off one set of emotions without affecting them all; the emotion nozzles are all inter-connected. Sure, I did not cry anymore, but neither did I laugh. My life turned into a flat, emotionless existence. I could not love. I had no passion. I had lost touch with joy. I was not sad, but I wasn't happy. I had the personality of a rice cake. I am so grateful that my husband made the commitment of "for better or for worse" and took it seriously, because this was definitely for worse. My attitude and emotional void also made me very lonely, which only compounded the problem.

Whenever I look at pictures from this time in my life, I am reminded how unhealthy it is to stuff emotions. The effects were evident in every picture of me; my eyes were dull, the smile forced and the body language defeated.

When we realize how far we drift from God in enduring trials, he will call us back into repentance. He did this form me when I read Psalm 103:10-17,

> "He does not treat us as our sins deserve or repay us according to our iniquities. For as high as the heavens are above the earth, so great is his love for those who fear him; as far as the east is from the west, so far has he removed our transgressions from us. As a father has compassion on his children, so the Lord has compassion on those who hear him; for he knows how we are formed, he remembers that we are dust. As for man, his days are like grass, he flourishes like a flower of the field; the wind blows over it and it is gone, and its place remembers it no more. But from everlasting to everlasting, the Lord's love is with those who fear him."

There is no place you can go to escape God's love

for you. He relentlessly pursues you as he did me. There is no sin you have committed against him that he will not forgive—even your anger or apathy cannot keep him away from you. He forgave me for blaming him for the death of my children. He never stopped loving me, even when I turned on him. He will never stop loving you, either.

When you reach out for him to take hold of your hand, he will show you exactly who he is, and what he can do.

Chapter 6 God's Truth > My Truth

You turn things upside down, as if the potter were thought to be like the clay! Shall what is formed say to him who formed it, "He did not make me"? Can the pot say to the potter, "He knows nothing"? Isaiah 29:16

God is serious about his authority over our lives. He wants our obedience and our faith. While he allows us to bring him our questions, this verse implies that we need to trust what he is doing in our lives whether or not we understand it. These are the lessons that God taught me when I returned to him. He strictly established his authority in my life so I could learn to trust him again.

Do you remember third grade math? We learned important things like fractions, multiplication and greater than/less than. I received a third-grade math lesson from God when he taught me those hard truths that I have summed up with the equation:

God's Truth > My Truth

Not only is God's truth always right, his way of thinking is also better than ours. For example, look at Luke 6:38, "Give, and it will be given to you. A good measure, pressed down, shaken together and running over, will be poured into your lap. For with the same measure you use, it will be measured to you."

I liken this verse to the process of measuring flour; when you measure it, you are supposed to scoop the flour from its container and pour it into the measuring cup. If you scoop the flour with your cup, you end up compressing the flour and pack too much in the measuring cup. Your baked food will be very dense as a result. Our perspective says, "scoop and pour" so we don't give too much. God's perspective says in effect, "When I measure, I'll shake the air out, pack it down and fill it until it's pouring over the edges." Cup for cup, God packs in more than we ever could!

During my renewed quiet times with God, he showed me where I was disregarding his authority and wisdom and living in my own strength and that if I continued in my own strength, I was doomed to failure. Like many facing hardship, my trials caused me to judge God by my circumstances and I devised my own theology based on what would make me more comfortable and happier. I learned how wrong it is to pick and choose what I believe about God. He showed me that if I was committed to following him, I had to do it on his terms, not mine—

not an easy lesson but a necessary one for healing.

Let me warn you, this chapter is full of some hard facts about God's authority in our lives, in addition to reasons why we should have a healthy respect for him and his authority. We don't like talking about why we need to respect God because instead we like to talk about his mercy and love. This is an easier pill to swallow. However, I firmly believe that we can't understand or appreciate God's love, mercy and grace until we understand his awesome power and authority as God Most High—Creator of the universe and all things in it and the one who controls all things for our good and his glory.

Together we are going to study God's truth, plain and simple. No sugar coating, no chocolate on the side (although a little dark chocolate couldn't hurt if you have some handy!); no flowery or feel-good phrases—just the fact that God is God and we are not. Accepting God for *who* he is and *how* he is was a pivotal point in my healing process. When I listened to what God's truth said about my life and circumstances, I grew in him, trusted him more, and had the strength to climb out of the valley I found myself in. This new understanding of God's almighty power and authority will strip away any selfish attitudes about God and replace them with truth. This unabashed truth caused my faith to change from loving God with conditions (as if he was a genie bound to do my bidding), to loving him for who he is, and for the mercy, grace and salvation he showers upon me.

Over a two-year time span, God patiently showed

me how and where my behavior and thoughts were contrary to his. I am praying he will speak to you in this chapter and that you will open your heart and allow him to continue his work in you. His word promises he will finish that work. Here I will revisit some of the attitudes I developed over the years I struggled through the valley of shadows; together we can see how God revealed his authority and perspective in those situations.

I tried in vain to run away from all of my pain by throwing myself into church activities. I've mentioned before what a hypocrite I had become—leading Bible studies, starting women's ministry, hosting small groups in our home, etc. God showed me what he thinks about "going through the motions"; in short, he abhors it. Learning his perspective helped our new relationship grow. As I ambled through the Old Testament, I stopped and studied Amos 5:21-24:

> I hate, I despise your religious feasts; I cannot stand your assemblies. Even though you bring me burnt offerings and grain offerings, I will not accept them. Though you bring choice fellowship offerings, I have no regard for them. Away with the noise of your songs! I will not listen to the music of your harps. But let justice roll on like a river, righteousness like a never-failing stream!

While studying this passage, I learned that the offerings the Israelites were burning to God were all optional fellowship offerings. They neglected and bypassed their sin offerings assuming they did not need it. Through this, I learned that God, although loving, is a hard master; we cannot presume our goodness in front of him; we must acknowledge our sin before him before we can have intimate fellowship with him. Additionally, the fellowship offerings are meaningless if they are not given with an honest heart. God desires relationship with us more than he wants empty actions. My actions—serving in the church when I was so angry—was just like those fellowship offerings. They were made halfheartedly and they took the place of a personal relationship with God.

God demands our whole-hearted devotion more than anything else. Isaiah records a monologue from God to the Israelites where he admonishes them for merely "going through the motions" regarding fasting. He accuses them of fasting only outwardly so others would see how pious they were. Yet, he says,

> "On the day of your fasting, you do
> as you please and exploit all your workers.
> Your fasting ends in quarreling and strife,
> and in striking each other with wicked
> fists. You cannot fast as you do today and
> expect your voice to be heard on high."
> (Isaiah 5:3b-4).

To have full reconciliation with God, we have to admit that it is he who made us, and not we who made him. We cannot make up our own rules to follow about God, because *he* is the rule maker. He has the authority to have authority in our lives. If he is the maker then we are the made, and we have no right to undermine his authority with rules and perceptions of our own.

Its not our job to tell God what is right or fair

To prove this point further, I have a note in the margin by Job 40:2; *it's not our job to tell God what is right or fair for only his way is righteous!* It is a response to the verse that reads, "Will the one who contends with the Almighty correct him? Let him who accuses God answer him!" Ouch. I don't think I want to be in that position. Do you want to hear what God said to Job before this? In chapter Job 38, God responds to Job's lament over his circumstances with questions of his own:

Where were you when I laid the earth's foundation...Who shut up the sea behind doors when it burst forth from the womb...when I said, "this far you may come and no farther"...Have you ever given orders to the morning, or shown the dawn its place...Have you entered the storehouses of the snow or seen the storehouses of hail which I reserve for times of trouble...Do you know the laws of the heavens or have you set up God's dominion on earth?...Do you send the lightning bolts on their way...Do they report to you, "here we are'?

These questions continue through chapter 41; it is a powerful read for certain, and I encourage you to consider everything God says he does in these chapters through your own study. Job did, and finally answered God with words similar to those I used when he drew me out of my pit; Job replied to God; "I know that you can do all things; no plan of yours can be thwarted…" Indeed.

Not only does he have the right to have authority over us, we have the obligation of obedience to him. When we refuse to be obedient, God will call us into account as he did to Moses. He was on his way back to Egypt in obedience to God's command but he had not been obedient in all things.

> At a lodging place on the way, the Lord met Moses and was about to kill him. But Zipporah took a flint knife, cut off her son's foreskin and touched Moses' feet with it. "Surely you are a bridegroom of blood to me," she said. So the Lord left him alone. Exodus 4:24-26

What? God was going to kill Moses for not circumcising his son? Is this harsh? Yes. Is it just? Yes. God is serious when he says he wants our obedience in all things. Here is what John Wesley's Explanatory Notes says about this verse:

> "The Lord met him, and, probably, by a sword in an angel's hand sought to kill him—This was a great change. Very lately God was conversing with him as a friend,

and now coming forth against him as an enemy."

So Zipporah circumcised the boy herself, appeasing the Lord with their obedience. Moses was about to go do something so great in the Lord—setting the Israelites free from Pharaoh—that the Lord could not stand even a hint of disobedience in Moses' life. There is probably application for us as well.

Later, when God gave Moses the Ten Commandments and other regulations, Moses warned the people, many times in fact, to remember the Lord.

> Be careful to follow every command I am giving you today, so that you may live and increase and may enter and possess the land that the Lord promised on oath to your forefathers. (Deuteronomy 8:1)

> Again, in 8:11 Moses said, "Be careful that you do not forget the Lord your God, failing to observe his commands, his laws and his decrees that I am giving you this day."

Don't you think he knew that by experience? Two chapters later in the same book of Deuteronomy, Moses was still talking about obedience to God.

And now…what does the Lord your God ask of you but to fear the Lord your God, to walk in all his ways, to love him, to serve the Lord your God with all your heart and with all your soul, and to observe the Lord's commands and decrees that I am giving you today. (Deuteronomy 10:12)

We daily need God's Mercy and his gift of Jesus

This reminds me of the verse in James 2:10 that reads, "For whoever keeps the whole law and yet stumbles in one point, he has become guilty of all." I wrote a note in the margin; *Because we cannot keep the law, we daily need God's mercy and his gift of Jesus.*

Another harsh reality about God is this: He is jealous of his position and he does not want us to put ourselves above him.

Woe to him who quarrels with his Maker, to him who is but a potsherd among the potsherds on the ground. Does the clay say to the potter, "what are you making?" Does your work say, "He has no hands"? Woe to him who says to his father, "what have you begotten?" or to his mother, "What have you brought to birth?" This is what the Lord says—the Holy One of Israel, and its Maker: Concerning things to come, do you question me about my children, or give orders about the work of my hands? It is I who made the earth and created mankind upon it. My own hands stretched out the heavens. I marshaled their starry hosts… (v. 21)…was it not I, the Lord? And there is no God apart from me, a righteous God and a Savior; there is none but me. Isaiah 45:9-12

I don't know about you, but I don't want any more woe! Jesus said a something similar in Matthew when he was preparing the disciples for persecution.

Matthew 10:32-39 says:

Whoever acknowledges me before men, I will also acknowledge him before my Father in heaven. But whoever disowns me before men, I will disown him before my father in heaven. Do not suppose that I have come to bring peace to the earth. I did not come to bring peace, but a sword. For I have come to turn, "a man against his father, a daughter against her mother, a daughter-in-law against her mother-in-law—a man's enemies will be the members of his own household," (from Micah 7:6). Anyone who loves his father or mother more than me is not worthy of me; anyone who loves his son or daughter more than

me is no worthy of me, and anyone who
does not take his cross and follow me is
not worthy of me.

God is pretty serious about our commitment to
him. He is also very serious about his commitment to
us. We don't talk about those harsh truths very much in
church, but I echo Moses when he kept saying, remember
the Lord and do what he says. I have found that when I
remember how holy God is, I'm more grateful for his
mercy towards me.

After these hard-hitting lessons, God was kind
enough to let me rest in gentler verses such as, "Many are
the plans in a man's heart, but it is the Lord's purpose that
prevails," from Proverbs 19:21. This reminded me that
my life was under the control and authority of God and
his plans for me would prevail. I was finally at the point
where I could pray—and mean—the note by the side of
this verse: *Let your purpose prevail in my life.* He also
encouraged me through many other verses that he will
bring me through my trials for his glory, to display his
splendor. He said he will provide for those who grieve and
bestow on them a crown of beauty instead of ashes (Isaiah
61: 3 paraphrased).

Next, God helped me understand what he expected
of me when I was upset that the women in Texas were
hurting and abandoning their precious babies; it was an
issue of his sense of justice and perspective being different
from mine. He started gently by showing me Proverbs

Let your pur- pose prevail

23:1-3,

It is better to die than to crave what some- one else has. Be con- cerned with what God gave you.

"When you sit to dine with a ruler, note well what is before you, and put a knife to your throat if you are given to gluttony. Do not crave his delicacies, for that food is deceptive."

At first glance, it looks like this verse is about overeating, but if you look more closely you will see what I did: Note what is before you and don't crave the delicacies others have because those delicacies are quite deceptive. The note in the margin of by Bible by this verse says, *it is better to die than to crave what someone else has—be concerned with what God gave you.* This verse can be taken two ways—don't covet the things of the world but instead be happy with you have, or in my case, don't be envious of others who have children—regardless of how they treat them; instead be concerned with what God has asked you to do with your life.

I obviously needed more information on this topic because a few weeks later Malachi 2:17 and 3:14 came to my attention.

"You have wearied the Lord with your words. 'How have we wearied him?' you ask. By saying 'All who do evil are good in the eyes of the Lord, and he is pleased with them' or, 'Where is the God of justice...You have said, 'It is futile to serve God. What did we gain by carrying out his requirements and going about like mourners before the Lord Almighty? But now we call the arrogant blessed. Certainly the evildoers prosper, and even those who challenge God escape.'"

This is only my limited view! God will work it out in the end.

Echoes of past conversations came to mind; *I'll just be a quiet Christian...What good has it done for me to follow him...Why should I follow him if all I get is pain... Those who don't want or love their children are blessed by God because they have children anyway.* God was showing me the error in my perspective. God is a God of justice, and in the end, he will work everything out according to our obedience to him. I wrote in the margin; *Repent of this! This is only my limited view; God will work it all out in the end.*

God, in his goodness and love, didn't leave it there. Next, he revealed Proverbs 23:17-18,

> "Do not let your heart envy sinners, but always be zealous for fear of the Lord. There is surely a future hope for you, and your hope will not be cut off."

I love the way this verse helped me not only let go of a wrong behavior, but revealed what to replace those

119

thoughts and wrong behavior with. When I let go of my envy, I can replace it with a zealous respect for God, and in that, I suddenly have a future hope that will not be cut off. If I don't fill up with something good when I let go of something sinful, I could succumb to continued and worsening sinful behavior.

Jesus told his disciples a story about this very subject.

> He said, "When an evil spirit comes out of a man, it goes through arid placed seeking rest and does not find it. Then it says, 'I will return to the house I left.' When it arrives, it finds the house unoccupied, swept clean and put in order. Then it goes and takes with it seven other spirits more wicked than itself, and they go in and live there. And the final condition of that man is worse than at first."
> Matthew 12:43-45

As he changed my perspective from my limited view to his omniscient view, God was always faithful to show me something positive that replaced the skewed perspective. I truly believe this very behavior is what saved my sanity. Recently, I was talking to a counselor and sharing this story with her. She was amazed because in her opinion, at that point (many years after these trials) I was emotionally very healthy. I give God the honor and glory for my emotional health because he taught me how to rid myself of an unhealthy attitude and replace it with things of God.

Sometimes we think that life doesn't make sense, and from our view, it doesn't. But from God's view, everything is working out just as he planned for it to. His view is just different from ours.

The Bible gives thousands of examples of how God thinks differently than we do. God himself says,

"For my thoughts are not your thoughts, neither are your ways my ways," declares the Lord. "As the heavens are higher than the earth, so are my ways higher than your ways and my thoughts higher than your thoughts." (Isaiah 55:8-9).

Jesse and his family thought it was crazy that David, the youngest and smallest of the clan, was anointed and chosen to one day rule as king. Everyone thought Noah was nuts when he started building the ark as God told him to. The sons of Jacob were amazed that their brother, who they sold as a slave, was the man who saved their family from certain starvation. When the Israelites wandered in the desert for 40 years, not one thread of their clothing was worn out because God said he would take care of it.

Even Jesus turned "approved religion" on its head when he said things like, "I tell you, love your enemy and pray for him," or, "If someone asks for your tunic, give him your cloak as well," and "You must be born again into eternal life." His message from the Sermon on the Mount was also counter intuitive; blessed are those who mourn... How can mourning be a blessing? His ways are not our ways; but his ways are truly better.

Sometimes, however, God's ways are harder to follow or understand. It's difficult to swallow mandates like, "You have heard it said, do not commit adultery, but I tell you that if you even look at a woman with lust in your eyes, you have committed adultery with her already in your heart" (Matthew 5:28). It's difficult to understand when God says that not everyone who calls on him will enter the kingdom of heaven. Matthew 7:21-23 is marked in my Bible:

> "Not everyone who says to me, 'Lord, Lord,' will enter the kingdom of heaven, but only he who does the will of my Father who is in heaven. Many will say to me on that day, 'Lord, Lord, did we not prophesy in your name, and in your name drive out demons and perform miracles? Then I will tell them plainly, 'I never knew you. Away from me you evil doers!'"

There are several notes in the margins by these verses. One highlights the importance of a daily relationship with Jesus. When I read those words, *I never knew you,* I was deeply saddened. In essence, he was telling those people that he never had a relationship with them. I did not want that to be me. Another note by that verse explains how we make sure Jesus knows us: *God created us so we can know him; we show we know him by obeying him; then he knows us.* Jesus then went on to teach about those who build houses on rock and sand. The Bible says that all those who were listening to him were amazed at his teaching because of his authority.

I am not a scholar, and there are literally thousands of sermons, texts and commentaries aimed and helping us understand these challenging decrees. All I know is that if we trust God for our salvation and blessings, hope and peace in our lives, we also have to trust him with these harder principles—and even the hard circumstances of life. We can't pick the easy way and ignore the hard way.

As hard as some of God's truths are, some are also downright confusing. For example, one day in my Bible reading I stopped at Isaiah 54:1,

> "Sing, O barren woman, you who never bore a child; burst into song, shout for joy, you who were never in labor; because more are the children of a desolate woman than of her who has a husband."

What!? This did not make any sense in the midst of my situation! How could my "children" outnumber those who can have children? After praying about this verse, I was finally able to write a note in the margin by this verse. At first, I thought maybe God was telling me that eventually I would have children. But God revealed that the heritage would be a Spiritual Heritage—since I don't have children, I can concentrate on helping women heal and be set free, to share and comfort them in their trials. I wrote in the margin, *spiritual heritage is more important to God than physical heritage.* Thus began my writing ministry.

It is a spiritual heritage!

Jesus talks about the process of changing our perspective as the process of being pruned. In John 11, he says that those who don't produce fruit for God are cut off and burned, and those who do produce fruit are cut back so their fruit can be bigger and better. Pruning can hurt. It often results from trials in our lives which, whether given by God or not, are there so that God can bring good from them. That pruning produces bigger fruit in our lives which leaves a spiritual heritage to those around us.

One final thought about this process of changing perspective from the pain of the circumstance to focusing on God; nothing is hidden from God's sight. Hebrews 4:13 says, "Nothing in all creation is hidden from God's sight. Everything is uncovered and laid bare before the eyes of him to whom we must give account." Yes, our unconfessed sins and shortcomings are visible to God, but so are our pain and our struggles. God is not distant or uncaring. He is just. He is merciful. And most of all, he loves his creation and works all things in this world for the good of those who love him to glorify himself. He wants us to live abundant lives in his love as we find our satisfaction in him. He even provides the way; according to Romans 10:9-13

> If you confess with your mouth, "Jesus is Lord," and believe in your heart that God raised him from the dead, you will be saved. For it is with your heart that you believe and are justified, and it is with your mouth that you confess and are saved. As the Scripture says, "Anyone who trusts in him will never be put to shame." (from Isaiah 28:16). For there is no difference between Jew and Gentile—the same Lord is Lord of all and richly blesses all who calls on him, for, "Everyone who calls on the name of the Lord will be saved." (from Joel 2:32)

Good News!

To me, this is good news. Although God does not joke around about his authority over our lives, he also gives us a way to live under his just sense of righteousness. When we trust in Jesus, we are saved from God's mighty wrath and proclaimed as his sons and daughters!

God's justice calls us to give up anything in our lives that is devoted to destruction and trust wholly in his power to save us. When we let go of our old ways and rest in God's character, we will be able to see and understand what an awesome God he is.

Chapter 7
An Awesome God

*T*his is what the Lord says—your Redeemer, the Holy One of Israel: "I am the Lord your God, who teaches you what is best for you, who directs you in the way you should go." Isaiah 48:17

Because God first tore down my false perceptions and showed me his truth forthright, I was prepared for the amazing awesomeness of his character. He helped me see that my perspective was not only invalid, but also a foothold of the devil. Then, when God showed me his unchanging character, I began to understand him better and deal with my circumstances in light of what I was learning about him. He is the one who directed me in the way I should go next.

Granted, this was not a magic pill that made everything bearable, but I eventually learned to view my circumstances according to his character. This made me more patient through my trials.

At the beginning of the time when God started teaching me about his multifaceted and magnificent character, I found out I was pregnant again. This was my eighth pregnancy; we lost one by my first tubal, then we lost Andrew because of the heart defect, and we lost five other pregnancies through miscarriage. I was a wreck. I struggled with whether or not I should tell Brandon—I didn't want him to worry needlessly, but I also did not want to deal with the stress alone. An overwhelming fear gripped me—I was so tired of losing babies! Trying to be responsible, I called my doctor, made an appointment for the next week, and told Brandon at the end of the day. He reacted much the same way I did; fighting off the fear for my life and dreading the loss of another child.

That night, I remember praying fervently about my pregnancy: *"God, I can't handle this pain anymore. We've tried so many times to have children and it hasn't worked. Tonight I'm praying that you will either allow this baby to survive, or take away my ability to have children."*

The next day I was working on some Bible study homework in Isaiah 41 when I was moved to keep reading past the assignment. My eyes rested on verse 41:13, "For I am the LORD, your God, who takes hold of your right hand and says to you, Do not fear; I will help you." I was stirred to tears—it was as if God was sitting across the table from me saying these words of comfort. He addressed my prayer from the night before in such a real way. I was instantly comforted and released from the fear; but I also knew deep inside that I would lose the baby because of the familiar pains I felt in my side.

One day later, I was leading a small group of women for Bible study when I felt a pop in my lower abdomen; I immediately broke out in a cold sweat and felt sick to my stomach from the pain. My mind raced back to all those years ago when I was standing in the lobby after church in Hawaii and felt that same pop in my gut—I was losing the baby and simultaneously God was answering my prayers by taking my last fallopian tube with it. I had gotten so used to silence from God regarding my pregnancies that I was surprised but oddly at peace with such an overt answer.

This time I knew what to do. I called Brandon home from work and a friend drove me to my house to meet him. Brandon drove me to the emergency room where he carried me in and told them my tube had ruptured. Interestingly, we were both very calm, as if God really was taking my by the hand and saying, "I will help you."

The nurses in the ER didn't know us from Adam, so they would not believe our "civilian" diagnosis. They admitted me, ran tests, and acted baffled over my symptoms. I was thankful that this ruptured tubal pregnancy did not seem as severe as my first. I was quite lucid and only had moments of such pain that I couldn't breathe or talk. Two hours later, as I was still laying on the bed in the ER, I noticed a new sharp, stabbing pain in my right shoulder. The technician left and came back with the head of OB-GYN. I can't remember his name, but as he read my record, he looked up and said, "I know about you!" *Great,* I thought, *I've become a case study.*

When I told the doctor I had a pain in my shoulder, he whacked the bottom of my feet with his hand. This increased my pain so much that I could only cry out, "OUCH!" The doctor started barking orders. "Prep the OR! Get some release papers for them! Get her admitted!"

It turns out the pain in my shoulder was from blood pooling in my abdomen and spilling into my upper cavity. The whack the doctor gave my feet confirmed for him that I was bleeding internally and they needed to move fast to save my life. Again. (As I write this, I am reminded that I am supposed to be here, for there were three times I almost wasn't! I know God has saved me to fulfill his purpose in my life).

Because this ruptured tube did not tear a major vein like my first tubal, they were able to complete this surgery with lasers. I was home that evening in a lot of pain, but with great emotional relief. It was over. Our friends, neighbors and church family came with meals and flowers, and God gave me peace.

Two days later, in the office of the OB-GYN at Wilford Hall in San Antonio, Texas, the head of the department told Brandon and me it was time to stop. He said many doctors would recommend couples move forward with invitro or other fertility treatments, but he told us not to. He thought that with my "train wreck" of a medical history, my many miscarriages, and the chances of having another child with a heart defect, that it was time for us to abandon that train wreck all together.

Over dinner that night, Brandon and I decided it was time to heal. It was a relief to be off the horrible emotional roller coaster that had tormented us for the past five years. We were eager to live again, without fear and without loss. We didn't rule out the idea of adopting, but we chose to not even talk about it for a year so we could fully heal and make a good decision about our family situation.

For the next three months while I healed from the surgery, God helped me heal emotionally and spiritually. He showed me through his word all of the good and amazing things he does for us, his creation. This was when I fell in love with God again.

> "This is what God the LORD says—he who created the heavens and stretches them out, who spread out the earth and all that comes out of it, who gives breath to its people, and life to those who walk on it; I, the LORD, have called you in righteousness; I will take hold of your hand" (Isaiah 42:5-6).

Indeed, he took hold of my hand and showed me all he could be for me when I trust and obey.

He started with some very personal aspects of his character that immediately kept me from falling back into the pit I had worked so hard to escape. I learned that God rescues and protects me, never lets me go and that saved my life for a reason. Psalm 18 says,

> "I call to the Lord, who is worthy of praise, and I am saved from my enemies. The cords of death entangled me; the torrents of destruction overwhelmed me…He reached down from on high and took hold of me; he drew me out of deep waters… He brought me into a spacious place; he rescued me because he delights in me" (verses 3, 4, 16, 19).

God can be such a personal God when we seek him to fill our deepest needs. When I needed a rescuer, he was there. When the cords of death entangled me, he reached down from on high and rescued me. Why? Because he delights in me!

This one amazes me the most. God delights in me! Even after I cursed him for taking away my babies. After I turned my back on him to entertain the devil. Even after every sin I commit every day—he still *delights* in me! That amazes me!

Even more than his delight, we are also his *treasure:* Deuteronomy 14:1 says, "The Lord has chosen you to be his treasured possession." The note in the margin by this verse says, *beyond measure.* God treasures me so much, it is immeasurable. Think about what you treasure the most on this earth...your spouse, kids, heirlooms, a bible verse, a gift...God treasures you more than that!

God's comfort, forgiveness and healing go hand in hand with us being his treasured possessions. Because he cares so deeply, he offers us comfort in our pain. Psalm 103 tells of God's forgiveness and healing:

> Praise the Lord, O my soul; and forget not all his benefits— who forgives all your sins, and heals all your diseases, who redeems your life from the pit and crowns you with love and compassion, who satisfies your desires with good things so that your youth is renewed like the eagles.

David wrote this Psalm—a man after God's own heart who also knew the devastation of sin and trials in life. The whole song sings the praises of what God is really like. When I read this Psalm, I exploded with a new and deeper love for God.

My husband, Brandon, has deployed many times since the war in Afghanistan and Iraq. When he is gone, we'll connect often by email, but for some reason it's those hand-written notes that we trade during those long months of separation that are the most meaningful to me. In those, he writes why he loves me. He explains why his love for me will never die. I cherish those notes because they are from his heart and written just for me.

Sometimes, the Bible—especially the Psalms—

seems like one of those love letters; written from the heart, just for me. But *these* love letters are from God showing me what I mean to him and how great and wondrous his love for me is. Psalm 104 exalts God for his provision and care of his creation. "These all look to you to give them their food at the proper time. When you give it up to them, they gather it up; when you open your hand, they are satisfied with good things" (Psalm 104:27-28). God provides for me and satisfies me when I accept his love for me.

I also learned that God has a distinct purpose for me and all of his children. One of the many proofs of this is in Ephesians 1:11:

"In him we were also chosen, having been predestined according to the plan of him who works out everything in conformity with the purpose of his will, in order that we, who were the first to hope in Christ, might be for the praise of his glory."

This purpose is not about me. It's not for my glory even my comfort—it is about God, who, for his glory and purpose, chose me to be here—at this place and time—to work out his will for me and those around me. Do you know what the most incredible aspect of living in God's purpose is? He fulfills it in me! All I have to do is show up, and be available and obedient.

Psalm 138:8 says,

"The Lord will fulfill his purpose for me;
your love, O Lord, endures forever—do
not abandon the works of your hands."

Amen!

Amen! We can have confidence in God's faithfulness to us because the Bible says, he who began a good work in you will carry it on to completion until the day of Christ Jesus (see Philippians 1:6).

God gives us everything we need to do the work he wants us to do. I love how it is written in 2 Peter;

> "His divine power has given us everything we need for life and godliness through our knowledge of him who called us by his own glory and goodness. Through these he has given us his very great and precious promises, so that through them you may participate in the divine nature and escape the corruption in the world caused by evil desires" (1:3-4).

If I had known this during those years of miscarriages, I wonder how it would have changed my attitude? If I knew more of God's nature and precious promises, I may have escaped the corruption of thought caused by the world. Who knows? Nonetheless, this knowledge now helps me during the challenges I have faced since I learned this concept.

During a trial, or grief or depression, it is easy to

be misled into thinking that the hard circumstance is just life and it is where we will spend the rest of our days. God wants so much more for us than that! He wants us to have a victorious and abundant life. He longs to give us good gifts (Matthew 7:11) and to be gracious to us (Isaiah 30:15). He loves those who seek him and allows himself to be found (Proverbs 8:17). But here is something that took me a long time to understand: God wants to give me more than what I ask for—exceedingly more than I could ask or imagine so I may be filled to the measure of all the fullness of God! (Ephesians 3:9-10)

In my depression and grief, I found myself begging God for a sip or a cup of water—I was so thirsty for him that I thought that maybe a sip of his water would satisfy me. I didn't feel like he was answering that prayer. What I learned is that God didn't want me to have just a sip—he wanted to give me the whole river.

A similar experience happened to a friend of mine (although I've changed her name here). Sarah was loosing her sight. In fact, at the young age of 32, she had already been declared legally blind. She wanted to try an experimental surgery, and prayed to God for the money to do it. Instead, she faced one financial burden after another, draining her bank accounts. She cried out to God, "Why don't you want me to see?!"

Sarah's sight never got better—and it never got worse. During her trial, she learned some lessons about her faith and about leaning on God. All the time she was begging for the experimental sight-saving surgery, it was like begging God for a cup of water. She thought she was thirsty for something and this cup of water would fill it. As she plodded through the financial burdens thrown her way, she started trusting God in new ways; to provide for her needs, to give her a place to live, to help her find a new job. The more she trusted in God, the more she saw *his* plan for her life.

This plan was like a river compared to the cup of water she was seeking. God's plan was one of faithful provision, abundant love and peace that passed any understanding. She firmly believes that if God had granted her the cup of water she was seeking, she never would have found the river that truly satisfied her need.

When our son, Andrew, was undergoing surgery for his heart defect, we desperately prayed that God would heal him. God took him instead. It took a long time to understand that the healing we asked for was like a cup of water. In taking Andrew, God gave us a river of peace simply because we didn't have to live in fear that each day Andrew lived might be his last. The survival rate for his particular problem is 50% from the surgery and each day. Each time he would have woken up, he would have had a 50% chance of living through the day.

God has planned something better for us... (Hebrews 11:40a). This verse is talking about replacing the promise in the covenant of the Law with the reality of the grace and mercy God gives us through Jesus. This verse also spoke something different to me the day I marked it in my margins. It spoke about the hope of something better.

God has planned something better for us!

God knows why Andrew died and why he chose for me to suffer from miscarriages; this verse promised me that in spite of those trials, God had something better in store for me—something beyond my understanding; something that took refined faith to see.

My strong personal relationship with God through Jesus is part of that something better. It's something that the Law could never give. Because of my relationship, I can rely on God's character, and even more than that, I can lean on him, trusting that he will walk with me through the trial and help me grow in him by the end.

I learned that God is bigger than my troubles—

> "You, dear children, are from God and have overcome (the trials of the world), because the one who is in you is greater than the one who is in the world" (1 John 4:4).

This is basically what David said as he went to face Goliath—the giant of a man who taunted and tormented the armies of Israel. He was a big monster of a man whose voice made strong, brave men shake in their armor. David didn't see the size of Goliath as a threat because he trusted in the size and strength of God. The same God you and I can lean on when our trials turn into Goliaths.

I believe that if we only call on God for salvation and never take the time to learn about who he is, we miss so much in a relationship with him. For example, if my mother always treated me as a child, our relationship would never have grown into a friendship as well. When I grew into an adult, she added that new dimension of being a friend and a confidant and because of that, I know her in such a different way now. Sure, she is still my mother, and she still reminds me to write my thank you notes after Christmas; but now, I can also talk to her about goals, dreams, challenges, friendships, relationships, and spiritual things; things that I would talk to a friend about. I am blessed by that.

We can be blessed in our relationship with God if we open our eyes and see him for everything he is. I carry around some index cards that remind me what I have learned about who God is. Some of those attributes from my note cards say that God:

- Carries me (Deuteronomy 1:31)
- Remembers me (Isaiah 49:15)
- Has compassion on me (Isaiah 40:1-5)
- Saves me, listens to me, forgives me (Psalm 86)
- Acts on my behalf (Isaiah 64:4)
- Abounds in steadfast love for me (Psalm 86:5)
- Is understanding (Psalm 147:4-5)

These truths about God's character are important for me to remember every day. They constantly remind me who God is so when things are hard and I can't see him, I can trust in his character. Circumstances come and go— they are ever changing. My God is not.

Psalms says that the Lord is faithful to all his promises and loving to all he has made (145:13); he watches over and hears those who love him. When we see his faithfulness and can trust that he hears us, we can lean on him with all our strength. Psalm 147:4-5 says that *WOW!* God "determines the number of the stars and calls them each by name. Great is our Lord and mighty in power, his understanding has no limit." I have "WOW" written in the margin by this verse. Every time I read this verse, I say wow!

Since we live in Colorado now, we have the chance to do more camping. I love getting up into the mountains where the morning air smells like pine trees and dirt, and the night sky shines so bright it seems like you could reach out and touch it. I have looked up at the night sky and wondered at the layers and layers of stars—so many they couldn't be counted. God made those! More than that, he has named each and every one of them. Do you realize that astronomers are still finding stars that haven't been discovered by man—but God knows each one intimately. Isaiah says that God brings out the starry hosts one by one and calls them each by name; Because of his great power and mighty strength, not one of them is missing (Isaiah 41:25).

Not only does he know the stars intimately, he knows us intimately as well. Each one of us! Psalm 139 says how our frames are not hidden from God, not even when we were being woven together in our mother's womb. We are not strangers to him. He relentlessly pursues us and desires to have a personal relationship with us. He wants to be more to us than a God who watches us from the distance. He wants us to be so close to him that we each call him *my* God. David often did that in the Psalms he wrote. He called God, My Rock, My Shepherd, and My Deliverer. I took a cue from David and starting calling on God as My Rock and My Deliverer. This is when my relationship with him grew even deeper.

When I am fighting off the dark places that people with depression and grief are haunted by, I call on God to become my sun and my shield from Psalm 84:11. God is my sun shining in the dark places to warm my weary spirit, and my shield to fight off the fiery darts of the devil who tries very hard to separate me from God again.

When I feel like I am slipping in quicksand or bombarded with waves of questions and doubts, God is my rock and strong fortress. When I need something solid to hold onto, he is there. When I need to stand on firm ground, he is there. When I need a place to hide, he is there. He is my ever-present help in times of trouble.

When I am distraught about not being able to bear children, God is my hope and satisfaction. This kind of hope is more than a wish, because a wish implies that something may or may not be. This hope, God Hope, is the knowledge that there is something better; I may or may not see it now, but I know I will have that something better for all of eternity. God is my satisfaction when I am unhappy and sad that my life-long wish of becoming a mother was not going to happen the way I thought it would.

God wants to be the fulfiller of all of my longings. He wants me to be like a tree planted by a river—with deep roots and no fear of drought. He wants me to bloom year-round and show a beautiful display of his splendor. And he will give me what I need whenever I call on him for it.

When my circumstances get the best of me and my days are filled with stress and strife, God is my peace and my rest. This knowledge allows me to take a step back and remember that this world is not really worth the value I sometimes put on it. What matters in the end is only my personal relationship with God.

One of the coolest things about a personal relationship with God is just that—it's personal. My relationship does not look the same as Brandon's, or my mom's or even your relationship with God. He personally knows what we need, and us and it is in his character to give to us when we seek him with pure, honest and cleansed hearts. God is not the same to all people—if he was, we would all have burning bush altars in our homes hoping that we would hear from God like Moses did.

Learning these character traits about God have helped me hang on to the good in times of trial (because trials don't stop—they just keep changing). Knowing this helps me "Faith" in God's character when I don't understand what he is doing.

Here is an example; I suffered from insomnia for about 2 ½ years, and I went back and forth between trusting that God would get me through it, and being angry at him for not taking it away. Then one day I remembered this lesson on God's character. I wrote out in my journal:

- I FAITH that God knows what I'm going through
- I FAITH that God will give me the strength to endure
- I FAITH that all things work together for the good of those who love Jesus

This didn't make my insomnia go away, but it kept my anger at bay because I was reminding myself that God is still in control, even when I didn't like what was happening. Because I pronounced faith in him through the trial, I was able to stand up under it.

Knowing all that God is capable of opened my eyes to the many ways God can help me through this life.

It also helps to know what God does *not* do so when the devil starts aiming his fiery darts at me, I can discern what is from God and what isn't.

From a personal study of Psalm 103, I can be sure that God does not treat us as our sins deserve....and for this I am so grateful. Knowing that I can come to God even after I have disobeyed or even cursed him for my circumstances, makes me very aware of his mercy and grace. My sins deserve death, but he does not give me death. Instead, he gives me love. In fact, the Psalm says, "as far as the east is from the west, so far has he removed our transgressions from us." God does not even harbor anger at us over our sins. The Bible says he chooses to forget them. (I have to wonder how different would our marriages and friendships be if we chose to forget the wrongs against us in those relationships?)

I can also be sure that God does not have a limit for his love for us. In both the Old and New Testaments, it is written that God's love for us is higher than the heavens, and deeper than the oceans, and there is no width, depth, or height that will ever separate us from his love.

Keep in mind; I am sharing with you in one chapter of a book what took me many months to understand during my "counseling sessions" with God. I encourage you to keep studying and seeking God for answers. He may not give them all, but he will give you what you need.

Going through this process of grieving, crying out, rebelling, repenting and learning about God's character is not a magic five-step process to clean out all of the sorrow in life. There are still going to be things about your struggles that you do not understand. There are things I still don't understand, so I'm waiting until I live in eternity with my Savior, who may explain it to me if it matters anymore. It may not matter.

If you have not felt excited about who God is through his character displayed in his past events, let me close with this writing from Isaiah sharing what God has in mind for our future. It just thrills my inmost being and makes me want to shout Hallelujah!

Behold, I will create new heavens and a

new earth. The former things will not be remembered, nor will they come to mind.

But be glad and rejoice forever in what I will create, for I will create Jerusalem to be a delight and its people a joy. I will rejoice over Jerusalem and take delight in my people; the sound of weeping and of crying will be heard in it no more.

Never again will there be in it an infant who lives but a few days, or an old man who does not live out his years; he who dies at a hundred will be thought a mere youth; He who fails to reach a hundred will be considered accursed.

They will build houses and dwell in them; they will plant vineyards and eat their fruit. No longer will they build houses and others live in them, or plant and others eat. For as the days of a tree, so will be the days of my people; my chosen ones will long enjoy the works of their hands.

They will not toil in vain or bear children doomed to misfortune; for they will be a people blessed by the Lord, they and their descendants with them. Before they call I will answer, while they are still speaking I will hear. Isaiah 65:17-24

AMEN! Now that is something to look forward to!

Chapter 8
Faith Refined by Fire and Fueled by Joy

*T*hough you have sent me troubles, many and bitter, you will restore my life again.
Psalm 71:2

God has deepened my faith, but even so, it is just the tip of the iceberg. I'm afraid that one chapter at the end of a book will not do the topic justice. So much has been written on faith, and there is still so much more to learn and say. I am by no means an expert on "all things of faith." I am no Billy Graham, Beth Moore or Kay Arthur; I'm just a woman who has been through a lot and learned some things about my faith. All I can share is what God showed me; the verses he used to deepen, strengthen and rebuild my faith.

In the previous chapters, God corrected some of my sinful and selfish attitudes and then showed me his true character from his word. I am convinced that a lesson on faith would never take hold until I could be confident in

God's character and trust what he says is true.

This journey to a refined faith started with 1 Peter 1:3-7, the verse he used to warn me of our impending journey into years of loss and infertility that I shared earlier. It is only right to revisit this verse again. Look at verses six and seven:

> In this you greatly rejoice, though now for a little while you may have had to suffer grief in all kinds of trials. These have come so that your faith—of greater worth than gold, which perishes, even though refined by fire—may be proved genuine and may result in praise, glory and honor when Jesus Christ is revealed.

Let's also look at verses eight and nine to complete the thought and see the reward that follows the trial:

> Though you have not seen him, you love him; and even though you do not see him now, you believe in him and are filled with an inexpressible and glorious joy, for you are receiving the goal of your faith, the salvation of your souls.

God allows trials and suffering to strengthen our faith—to refine and purify it so our faith is more precious to us than gold. Why is this kind of faith essential? Genuine faith is important to God because it brings us closer to him. I don't think he loves handing us trials, but he does love it when we lean more heavily on him and pursue the hope that there is purpose to our pain.

If my faith is based only on the good things God does for me, then it is conditional faith only. If I am faithful through my trials and I grow and learn, I become devoted to him who gives me the strength to endure. God wants our total devotion in good times and in bad. He wants our faith to be based on more than our condition.

Faith is simply trusting that God is right; that what he says is true and that what he does is righteous. I have mentioned before that at times I stopped trusting in God's character and faithfulness. I still relied on him for my eternal salvation, but I stopped trusting that he was doing the right thing with me. Lies from the deceiver took over my thoughts and I began to doubt God's righteousness. I was so hurt by my circumstances that I began to lose my faith (because it was conditional). Instead of burning with anger towards me, God used my weakness as an opportunity to purify my faith. He used it to prove to me that he cares about my *life*, not just my salvation.

With repeated doses of truth, God softened my heart with his word. I know, it sounds odd to say that on one hand, I had lost my faith and on the other, I was reading the Bible, but it was the only place I knew that would have the answers I was seeking. Because I turned to God for my healing instead of away from him in anger, my Spirit made me yearn for the word. I needed to discover the truth so I could stop living on the fence of knowing God but not trusting him.

God lovingly taught me about the kind of faith he wanted from me. Real faith. Refined faith. Faith based on the truth and righteousness of God and not on my circumstances. And I am so thankful.

The first dose of truth came with the words of Jesus in the Gospels. "Immediately, Jesus reached out his hand and caught him (Peter). 'You of little faith,' he said, 'why did you doubt?'" Matthew 14:31 *Peter was walking on water, and yet Jesus called him one of little faith?! These were the disciples who walked with him!*

And just a little bit further in the same book:

*Ye of little faith?
These were the disciples!*

He (Jesus) replied, "Because you have so little faith. I tell you the truth, if you have faith as small as a mustard seed, you can say to this mountain, 'Move from here to there,' and it will move. Nothing will be impossible for you" (Matthew 17:20).

The disciples were asking Jesus why they couldn't heal a certain man, and that was his reply: You have so little faith. *They were the Apostles!* These men lived with Jesus. They performed miracles! Moreover, to say that Peter—the rock, who vowed to stand by Jesus until the end—the first disciple to proclaim Jesus' deity—had *little faith!* It is more than I can comprehend even as I write this. Jesus said that faith the size of a mustard seed—about the size of a period at the end of a sentence, would be enough to move mountains. Yet the disciples did not even have that much.

I thought I had been so faithful to God during my years of sorrow, and yet God was telling me first off that I knew nothing about faith.

So what kind of faith does God require? How do we come about this faith? This is not a faith based on abilities or circumstances. This is faith based solely on God; only on his character and on his promises. That is why a lesson on faith cannot come before a lesson on God's character. If we don't know his character, we have nothing to base faith upon. Once we have that faith, God wants us to be confident in it:

> So do not throw away your confidence; it will be richly rewarded. You need to persevere so that when you have done the will of God, you will receive what he has promised. For in just a very little while, "He who is coming will come and will not delay. But my righteous one will live by faith. And if he shrinks back, I will not be pleased with him." But we are not of those who shrink back and are destroyed, but of those who believe and are saved (Hebrews 10:36-39).

Faith pleases God. True faith; based on him alone.

It shows God that we are willing to trust him. I had come to a place where my faith was based on whether or not God would allow me to have children. When I continually miscarried, my faith grew weak. Because my faith grew weak, I stopped believing in God's love for me. When I stopped believing in his love, I jumped into a pit of depression. Then, I couldn't hear from God because my faith was based on circumstances, not on him. He was waiting for me to see that.

Don't throw away your confidence. This verse says it all; if confidence is based on *our* understanding or *our* circumstances, it's like throwing it away. The confidence is worthless because it's based on a circumstance that will change; burn up like chaff and blow away.

Ten years ago, God warned me that I would face trials, but promised that he would not leave me alone in them. When I had faith in that promise, I endured and persevered. When I stopped believing that God was still with me and started relying on my own strength to overcome my circumstances, I crumbled. If faith is based on anything but God, it does not bear the load. Only faith in God's promises and character can stand up to the test of a fiery trial.

God doesn't change; when the confidence to overcome is based on God, it is secure. In that security we have a reward—we will receive what he has promised. That promise is the hope and faith revealed in the person of Jesus Christ. Do not shrink back from that faith; it is a gift from God! Shrinking from faith displeases God as much as having no faith grieves him. Living in faith—trusting that God is in control—brings him the glory he demands and deserves. It also helps us take the next step forward.

> And as soon as the priests who carry the ark of the Lord—the Lord of all the earth—set foot in the Jordan, its waters flowing downstream will be cut off and stand up in a heap (Joshua 3:13).

Take the step of faith before God has shown himself...

The lesson from this verse, written in the margins of my Bible is: *Take the step of faith, before God has shown himself, believing he will do as he said.* The third chapter of Joshua provided the instructions for crossing the Jordan when Joshua and the Israelites finally reached the Promised Land. The Jordan River, overflowing from the spring rains, was the last barrier between God's people and their Promise.

Imagine coming up to that river, flowing fast and furious over its banks. You are carrying your tent and all your household goods and the priests are carrying the Ark of the Covenant before you. The Lord has promised Joshua that as soon as the priests walked into the Jordan, the water would stop flowing and the people would have safe passage across this river (which could have been up to 15 feet deep and up to a half-mile wide). Apart from Joshua and Caleb, this generation of Israelites did not see Moses part the waters of the Dead Sea when the slave nation was escaping Pharaoh's wrath during their flight from Egypt. This generation, including the priests, has only heard the stories.

My Jordan River was believing that God's plan for me was better than what I wanted. It was the barrier standing between me and God's promise for me. In my finite mind, God was quite mistaken that I should not have biological children. After all, all I ever wanted in life was to be a mom. Wrapping my head around the fact that I would never bear my own children was a big, deep and wide barrier.

If you read on in this story, you will see in verses 15 and 16 that God was true to his word. As soon as the priests stepped into the water, the river stopped flowing and started piling up. The water receded for as long as it took the nation to cross on the dry ground. They were not even in the mud! It was dry ground! That's what God wants us to do—cross the barrier in faith, knowing that with him, we won't be stuck in the muck of the river bottom, but instead we will cross easily on dry ground.

But we have to take the step first. When we do, God will reveal himself and pile up the rushing waters so we can cross safely. God told Joshua he would do it, and he is true to his word. If he says he will do something, he is capable of doing it.

This was my next lesson: believing *that* God is capable. I meditated on Jeremiah 17:14:
Heal me, O Lord, and I will be healed: save me and I will

be saved, for you are the one I praise (Jeremiah 17:14). I marked in the margin; *I have to believe that God is capable and that he will do it.*

It is easy to say, "I believe in God." In fact, most Americans will tell you, whether they go to church or not, that they believe *in* God. Even the demons believe in God and shudder (James 2:19). Believing *in* God is very different than believing *that* God...

God is capable!

that God is capable
that God is willing
that God is loving
that God is interested
that God is _____ (fill in the blank)

Believing in God acknowledges the one greater than all things. Believing *that God* is trusting him to accomplish something in your life. It is trusting that he will do (and even has done) what he has said. Believing *that God*... is a step forward in faith.

It took me a long time to believe that God really did have a better plan. It took even longer to believe that God would heal me; I found myself defaulting back to my circumstances and the many times God did not allow my body to carry my pregnancies. I *wanted* to be healed emotionally and physically. I was tired of hurting and losing. I was tired of being strong. I read this verse; "Heal me, O Lord, and I will be healed..." and I *wanted* it to be so. I knew God *could* heal, but I doubted that he *would* heal me.

It is the second part of this verse that actually helped me have faith in the first. *"Save me and I will be saved."* I knew this part. My spirit knew that this was truth. I asked God to save me from the punishment of my sins through the death of Jesus on the cross, and I know he did. As evidence, I've had times of unexplainable peace, even a lack of fear, each of the three times I nearly died. I know that I know that I will be with Jesus in heaven when he does take me home. Since God doesn't let us pick and choose what we believe out of the Bible, I had to trust in the whole verse: "Heal me and I will be healed." If God said so, it would happen.

God did heal me, but not the way I would have chosen at the beginning of my trials. He healed me in more amazing and miraculous ways. He healed me from miscarriages by rendering my tubes useless, not to mention one time that he made the bleeding and pain disappear in an instant. He healed me from depression by building my faith. He healed me from a miserable, selfish, complacent life by showing me how to take my thoughts off myself and instead to dwell in him. His healing continues whenever I seek it because since he said it, it will be so.

God always promises something better for us, but we have to let go of what we are hanging on to and grasp what he wants to give us; we have to be willing to stretch and grow a little bit to find it. We have to be willing to sing, even in the midnight hour.

> About midnight Paul and Silas were praying and singing hymns to God, and the other prisoners were listening to them. Suddenly there was such a violent earthquake that the foundations of the prison were shaken. At once all the prison doors flew open and everybody's chains came loose (Acts 16:25-26).

I remember sitting in our little church in Texas when I read this verse. A midnight hour…that is what my life had felt like for years! The darkness felt so heavy around me. There was no light—no moon and no stars in sight. I was getting used to the darkness, even comfortable in it. I was ready to let it cover me up and then I read this; pray and sing! *What in the world is worth singing about in these circumstances?*

This is where faith has to step in. It is faith that gives hope. It can even put the song in your heart. Faith says, "God is still here. He wants to loosen your chains, make the walls around you tumble down and set you free from your dark prison." Faith is the only way I had the strength to sing. And so I did—but not aloud, mind you.

I tried that once years ago when I was grieving over Andrew and crying out to God. I had read in a prayer study that singing hymns to God brought an uncommon worship experience to the prayer time. So I sang. Then my dog started howling and crying with me. I don't think that is the uncommon experience the author intended!

That dog had often been my source of joy during those years so I was confused about his response to my song. I stopped my song short thinking the dog's crying was a sign that my singing was so bad that I shouldn't even offer it to God.

Looking back, I really hope the dog was offering praise with me in joyful abandon. I don't really know, but I do know that God loves any act of worship we offer whether or not it is in tune—as long as it is from the heart. Still, in this midnight hour, I sang God's praises in my head where they sounded much better before my throat got hold of them.

Singing praises and prayers to God in trial is really a sacrifice—it takes faith to praise God despite the hardship. But that sacrifice loosens our chains. It takes our eyes off our circumstances and by faith puts them on the one who brings peace. Sometimes I was so desperately overwhelmed by the darkness that there was not a single joyful note to be found. I quickly learned how to solve that problem; by playing praise and worship songs on my stereo (way before the days of the iPod, if you can believe it). I figured the devil could not bother me if I was busy praising God. And guess what? It worked! I soon saw a light in the darkness that grew until it overcame the darkness. Worshipping and praising God in song brought me right into the everlasting light of Christ.

These songs of praise and prayer in the midst of trial also have a profound impact on those around us. If you investigate this verse further, you will read that after the earthquake, the guard in charge was about to kill himself because he thought all the prisoners had escaped. "We're all here!" cried Paul. The songs of praise to God caused the prisoners around Paul to stay in the presence of God, to have peace in the midst of their circumstances. Even though the chains were loosened, the people remained where they were, fixed by the presence of God.

Please don't think I am saying that when you have been loosed from your chains that you need to stay in your trouble. I am not saying that at all, because when we are seeking God at the midnight hour, we will know what to do next.

Only God knows our next step, and it's up to us to seek it from him; sometimes it will be choosing to sing and pray despite our circumstances so he can break our chains. Sometimes God will ask us to just continue in the trial, without giving us freedom or the ability to understand it. This is the ultimate test of faith; believing anyway.

This verse is an epitaph of our trials; the verse and the notes are applicable here because there is an important faith lesson in them.

> All the ways of the Lord are loving and faithful for those who keep the demands of his covenant. For the sake of your name, O Lord, forgive my iniquity, though it is great. Who then, is the man that fears the Lord? He will instruct him in the way chosen for him. He will spend his days in

prosperity, and his descendants will inherit
the land (Psalm 25:10-13).

ectopic 5/95,
Andrew 8/30-9/14/96,
miscarriages: 5/97, 10/97, 4/98,
11/98, 4/99
5/00 last tubal; the end.
How can my descendants inherit
the land?

Some things in life are inherently difficult to
understand. Why do bad things happen to good people?
Why do God's people hurt? Why did this happen to me?
There are many things in my life, and yours too, that are
just hard to wrap your head around in the context of what
you know about God. My Sunday school teacher calls
these, "Faith Spots."

A Faith Spot is something in your life that hurts, is
hard, or just won't go away. They take more understanding
than you have in your own strength. These things take
divine trust; faith to believe that God will just work his
good out for them or that he will be present and help you
deal with them. These circumstances make us remember
how much we need God.

A child's death. A house fire killing an invalid
mother you cannot rescue. Terminal or chronic illness. The
untimely death of a loved one. Overcoming child abuse,
neglect or substance abuse. So many things hurt and so

many things are hard to endure.

I believe God leaves these Faith Spots in our lives so we will rely on his power. Sometimes, just like the Apostle Paul and the persistent thorn in his side, God wants us to feel our weakness. I don't think he does this out of cruelty (that is against his character). I think he does it so we will remember how to lean on him.

Can you define a Faith Spot in your life? Is there something that is still so hard to deal with that you have scratched it to death? Is it still an open sore? Let it heal. Then let it scar. God can use that scar to remind you of his power and his strength—the same power and strength that created the world. It is the same power and strength that he will supply for you every time that Faith Spot is rubbed.

A Faith Spot strips faith down to the very basics where we choose to follow God not because of the blessing He might give, but because of what he has already done on the cross through the blood of Jesus. Because God, out of love, stripped me of my selfishness and my perceptions, and clothed me in a beautiful newfound faith in him, I can accept challenging circumstances. I can live with Faith Spots because I've learned to hold them up to the light of God's word and his character. I work to understand them in his perspective, not my own. There are still some things that do not make sense to me, but I can learn to live with them because I trust God's decision.

It is these Faith Spots, where we have peace despite difficult circumstances, which cause the people around us to wonder where we get our strength. They cause us to be noticed not because of our complaining, but because of our confidence. They give us the opportunity to share with others what God is doing in the midst of our hardship. They also give us the opportunity to experience the greatest gift after a trial—Joy.

Faith and joy go hand in hand. Joy is more than simply being happy; it is a deep-rooted feeling of peace and contentment despite hardship or challenge. Faith brings joy; and joy brings purpose back to life.

Until God showed me the joy that comes from refined faith, I was living a dismal existence. I still do not like to look at photos from those years in my life because you can see in my face and my eyes that there is so much pain.

I heard somewhere that there are 365 references to "do not fear" in the Bible (one for each day of the year). I did a word search for joy in *The Bible in Basic English* on e-sword, and it came up with 377 references—enough for every day of the year and then some!

Here is one of my favorites; "He who goes out weeping, carrying seeds to sow, will return with songs of joy carrying sheaves with him" (Psalm 126:6). I love how this image implies that our tears will water the seeds we sow in sorrow, and one day we will return with songs of joy and armloads of fruit (or sheaves). It is true. When I look into my past from this vantage point, I can see fruit from the seeds that all of those tears watered. Fruit in my strengthened faith, fruit in my testimony of God's love, and fruit as the faith of those around me flourished.

It is appropriate that we are back in the Psalms for most of the discussion of joy—Psalms is definitely one of the most emotion-driven books of the Bible. I sat here a long time in sorrow, but now I'm dancing in the Psalms with joy. I have joy because I trust in God's plan for me, and I trust in his character. I know that weeping may remain for a night, but rejoicing comes in the morning (Psalm 30:5b). There was a long night of weeping in my life, but God has brought me out of the night, into the dawn of a new day. In the sunlight of this new day, I rejoice. He has turned my wailing into dancing; he removed my grieving clothes and clothed me with joy (Psalm 30:11). My heart cannot be silent! I give thanks and glory to God for bringing me through whole! I am grateful he did not abandon me in the darkness, but sought after me and molded me into something he can use.

God has made clear to me the way I should go, and telling this story has been big step in that direction. Being in his will has made my joy complete, *in his right hand there are pleasures forever and ever (Psalm 16:11).* Life has not always been easier living it under God's authority, but there has been much more peace than when there was without him. This fact is not only true for me, but true in history as well.

The history of the nation of Israel is a rocky one. I am no scholar by any stretch of the imagination but I've recently gained some insight while considering how God can turn our wailing into dancing and fill us with joy instead of sorrow. The Old Testament books of 1st and 2nd

Chronicles give a history of the kings of Israel. Some were godly, others were rotten. Whenever a godly king came into power after the nation had suffered in the hands of rotten kings, there was always much joy and rejoicing. The Israelites were oppressed and lost when the king did not follow God, but always relieved when they were led back to him.

I think this applies to the journey in the valley of the shadow of death—the grief we experience over loss or trials in our lives. When we are in the midst of a trial and turn from God out of anger or frustration, we live in darkness. Soon, we become accustomed to the darkness and feel comfortable there. However, when someone turns on a light and we see there is more to life than what we are experiencing, we respond with joy!

Here are some more examples from Psalms:

51:8   Make me full of joy and gladness; let the bones you have crushed rejoice.

51:12   Restore to me the joy of your salvation and grant me a willing spirit to sustain me!

59:16   But I will sing of your strength, in the morning I will sing for joy of your love, for you are my fortress, my refuge in times of trouble.

63:7   Because you are my help, I will
sing (joy) in the shadow of your wings.

I have just recently learned that the Hebrew word for wings
in this verse is the same word for character—which was a
good lesson for me; because of God's help, I can sing for
joy resting under his character.

    We can have joy at the end of our trials because
we've grown through them. We draw closer to God, we
become a help for others who have suffered, and we can
bask in the light of God's enduring love for us. Remember,
the joy of the Lord is our strength!

Chapter 9
What Now?

*J*esus said, "Go home to your family and tell them how much the Lord has done for you, and how he has had mercy on you. So the man went away and began to tell in the Decapolis how much Jesus had done for him. And all the people were amazed. (Mark 5:19-20)

In the New Testament, whenever Jesus interacted with people—especially when he healed them (except for a few times), he would say to the healed, go tell others what has happened to you. If you have let God reach you through this book, it is important to heed those words. It would be sad to have come this whole way to simply embrace the joy of the end of the trial and walk away with a nice feeling inside. If that is where the journey stops, you may soon find yourself back where you started, working through another journey of trials.

I have a note in the margin by Mark 5:19 (above); *It is a personal story...our faith is renewed and grows because of how God interacts in my life on a personal level.* This revelation helped me understand that to keep quiet about how God has healed me through my process of grieving, and in the challenging circumstances in my life, would be like forgetting to say thank you. There is a story in Luke about this subject.

It's a personal story...

As he was going into a village, ten men who had leprosy met him. They stood at a distance and called out in a loud voice, "Jesus, Master, have pity on us!" When he saw them, he said, "Go, show yourselves to the priests." And as they went, they were cleansed. One of them, when he saw he was healed, came back, praising God in a loud voice. He threw himself at Jesus' fee and thanked him—and he was a Samaritan. Jesus asked, "Were not all ten cleansed? Where are the other nine? Was no one found to return and give praise to God except this foreigner?" The he said to him, "Rise and go, your faith has made you well."

The story implies that I need to outwardly praise God for his work in my life; this shows my faith which will make me well. I don't know about you, but I want to continue being well. I have had enough darkness, sickness and death in my life. I want to stay close to God, abide in him, and continue to live in his will.

In my study, God showed me a few ways that I should continue in my relationship with him. I think it is important that I share them with you. The first one is about growing.

> Finally brothers, we instructed you how to
> live in order to please God, as in fact you
> are living. Now we ask you and urge you
> in the Lord Jesus to do this more and more
> (1 Thessalonians 4:1).

As much as God loves us the way we are, he also wants us to grow to be more like Jesus; more like the beautiful person *he* sees within us. Faith is not something that happens and you get over it. It's a process, not an achievement. We may start out as children who understand little, but he wants us to strive to understand more deeply, to become more confident in who he is and who we are in him. He wants our faith to be a verb—an action that is continually moving forward and upward. When we live this way, we can depend on God to give us exactly what we need to grow.

God uses our trials to help us grow. When something happens in life that is too big to understand and too big to handle alone, we learn to lean on God. In each new trial, we have an opportunity to experience God in new and bigger ways. We discover new facets of his vast character as it applies to the situation. As a result, we begin to see a bigger picture; we can see God as more than creator and we can start to rely on him in the many character traits he portrays to us. The more we turn to him, the more we trust him and the deeper our faith grows. The result is a life that is not only actively seeking God and growing, but also actively experiencing his love.

God gave us his word—the Bible—to help us understand him. When I see the way he works in the Bible, or even in the lives of others, I can trust him in new ways. I can more easily see the stability of his character, which gives me the hope, even the confidence, that he will be those things in my need.

When I read the Bible, I'm always amazed how a verse can mean one thing to me in one season and then something entirely different the next time I read it—and it can even have a different application to the person sitting next to me. The more you study a verse, the deeper you understand it. The more you read the Bible, the more of an impact it has on you. Please don't ever think that because you have read the Bible at one time in your life that it has nothing to teach you. God's word will not return void (Isaiah 55:11), He will always teach you as long as you study. As long as you study, you will keep growing in your personal faith. Psalm 1:1-3 confirm this:

Blessed is the man who does not walk

in the counsel of the wicked or stand in the way of sinners, or sit in the seat of mockers. But his delight is in the law of the Lord, and on his law he meditates day and night. He is like a tree planted by streams of water, which yields fruit in season and whose leaf does not wither. Whatever he does prospers.

I can see how God personalized my Bible through my trials through the notes in the margins. This has been paramount to my spiritual growth. Writing my thoughts, pains, hopes and fears and even the lessons I had learned made them easier to remember. Journaling allows me to express my emotion, understand my circumstances and concentrate on my prayers. My journals mark what I have learned and how far I had come and even helped me see God's healing process that now I am sharing with you.

I have mentioned before that our memories are short and we soon forget what God has done. I have gloried in an answered prayer but not written it down and then fought the same battle months later, forgetting how God would act in the situation. Writing it down helps me remember, which in turn feeds my faith.

See, experience and remember God's glorious presence in your life! Then, when the trials come again, you will have a head start because you'll know what God can do and you will already be grounded on the firm foundation of God's truth.

When we commit to spiritual growth, we will learn what is from God, and what is not. We will be able to discern what is happening in our lives, and know what to do about it. We will discover new and wonderful things about God and life that we did not know before.

> "Then, we will no longer be infants, tossed back and forth by the waves, and blown here and there by every wind of teaching and by the cunning and craftiness of men and their deceitful scheming" (Ephesians 5:14).

The point of our refined faith is bringing glory to God; to have so much peace in difficulty, and joy regardless of our circumstances that people ask, "What makes you so different?" Then we share God's goodness, love, compassion and mercy when we tell our story.

If we do not talk about what God has done, we will forget and we will be doomed to repeat the lesson. Remember in Joshua 3 how the Israelites had to step into the water by faith? They would not have had to courage to walk into a flooding river if their ancestors had not shared the glory of God; "We have heard how the Lord dried up the water of the Red Sea when you came out of Egypt," (Joshua 2:10). They could not have been confident in God's faithfulness if they did not know his character. They would not have known his character unless others told the stories.

These stories of God's work in our life helps not only us, but others understand his character. If we persevere but don't talk about the strength we receive from God to do so, we actually deceive people into thinking the strength comes from ourselves. When we don't point to God, others will think they should handle their problems alone and thus be doomed to failure. None of us can do it alone!

"Okay," you say. "I'm willing to talk about God, but what do I say?" More than anything, whatever you say is a personal story because we have a personal God. Our faith in God is not based on rules or hearsay. Our faith in God is proven by his personal interest in our lives—it's a relationship. No one can refute your relational experiences with God.

The man in the verse at the beginning of this chapter (from Mark 5) was healed of demon possession. The people of his town were still afraid of him, so the man wanted to go with Jesus. Jesus told him instead to tell his family and friends all that Jesus had done. No one would have believed that this man, who had terrorized a town because of the legion of demons that possessed him, was healed, unless they heard it from his own mouth.

Our words and our changed lives speak volumes to those in pain by offering hope and peace to the suffering. Our testimonies of coming out of the darkness and into the light give the hope of healing to those living in pain. The same kind of healing we have received from God. It cannot be kept secret! Let's start shouting it from the mountain top—yes the mountaintop on which God has placed you after faithfully walking you through your valley of shadows—and tell everyone how much the Lord has done for you! I, like Paul prayed for Philemon, pray that you may be active in sharing your faith, so that you will have a full understanding of every good thing we have in Christ (Philemon 1:6).

Finally, it is important to help others get through their grief. Proverbs 11:25 says, "A generous man will prosper; he who refreshes others will himself be refreshed.

As I was gaining back my equilibrium after exiting the roller coaster of childbearing challenges, my mother encouraged me to get involved in helping others who were going through similar experiences. Little did I know then how Biblical her advice was. When we reach out to help others, we will be helped. When we share joy with others, we receive joy. When we refresh others, we will in turn be refreshed. This principle is much like a hug; even if you are the one in need of it, you won't receive a hug until you give one.

I have a note in the margins by 2 Corinthians, chapter 1 where Paul is talking about the comfort we receive from God in our trials. The note says, *comfort people in the way I have felt God's comfort as a way of bringing good from the grief and sharing his love with others.* A good lesson for sure.

Paul, in his writings to the Corinthians, tells us we are a letter from Christ to the world. By our actions and our love, we help ignite the Spirit of the living God in others lives. We are still on this earth, instead of being taken up when we first believe, on Christ's authority with the mission to share with others as his love letter to the world.

Offer com- fort to others

When we help others, it builds relationships, fosters family and glorifies the Lord. Don't you want to be a part of that?

Now it is time for you to look back at the Notes in Your Margins. What is God telling you? How is he healing you? What will you do next? As for me, it is time to begin my next journey.

In the meantime, I will pray for you what Paul prayed for the Ephesians:

> ...I kneel before the Father, from whom his whole family in heaven and on Earth derives its name. I pray that out of his glorious riches he may strengthen you with power through his Spirit in your inner being, so that Christ may dwell in your hearts through faith. And I pray that you, being rooted and established in love, may have power, together with all the saints, to grasp how wide and long and high and deep is the love of Christ, and to know this love that surpasses knowledge—that you may be filled to the measure of all the fullness of God. Now to him to is able to do immeasurably more than all we ask

or imagine, according to his power that is at work within us, to him be glory in the church and in Christ Jesus throughout all generations, for ever and ever! Amen (Ephesians 3:14-21).

Many blessings in your journey!

Remember to check out my blog:
www.notesfromthemarginsbook.com

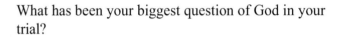

Comparing Notes:

The following questions are for personal application or group discussion. They are intended to help you dig deeper into your soul to help you find God's healing for your pain.

Introduction:

What has been your biggest question of God in your trial?

Does God Hear?

Does God See?

Does God Care?

Other

What is your current relationship with God?

Chapter 1: An Accidental Journal

When we write down the things that God does in our lives, we can readily see his hand at work and more easily recognize his warnings and his help. Are you a note taker or journaler? If so, what have you learned through your note taking? If not, why not?

What is the nature of the trial you are currently facing?

What is your impression about how God sees your trial?

Do you have a testimony from when you realized you needed God's salvation?

If not, did you pray the prayer at the beginning of the book? If you did, please share that information with a trusted friend and/or church leader.

Chapter 2: Days of Darkness

If we pitch our tent in the valley of the shadow of death, we will never grow from our trial. Instead, we will become used to the darkness and forget that there is light. Are you currently living in the dark? Describe it.

Sometimes it helps talking about the situation that brought you into the darkness—if you feel comfortable share the details about your trial with your group or with a trusted friend.

How has this trial affected your marriage?

Is there any verse God has shown you to prepare you or sustain you through your trial?

What questions swirl in your head about your trials?

Chapter 3: Existing Through the Grief

It is okay for Christians to experience grief and sorrow—Jesus did. I'm sure God has. Just because you are a person of faith does not mean you can avoid grief, or that you should ignore it. What being a Christian in grief does is give you God to help you through it. What was your first reaction to your hard situation...did you question, curse, turn to God?

What, if anything, has made it difficult for you to trust God right now?

Can you share a time where God met you in your grief?

What stupid things have others said to you while trying to help?

Is there a verse, chapter, or book of the Bible that is helping you through this trial?

Chapter 4: Crying out to God

God has heard it all! Nothing you can say or even yell at him will surprise him. He wants us to come to him with our questions so he can help us through them. What is your complaint to God?

Have you cried out to him?

Has he answered? How?

What are you afraid to cry out to God?

What do you think he might say?

Chapter 5:
When the Devil Came for Tea

When trials seem never ending, it is easy to become discouraged and doubt God's presence in your life. Our doubt gives the devil a foothold to help draw us away from God. Don't listen! Have your circumstances gotten the best of you?

Have you let the devil deceive you? How?

God told me, "Give careful thought to your ways." What is he telling you?

Of what should you repent? Did you?

Have you felt God's healing?

Have you, like I did, turned off all of your emotions to rid yourself of one? How has is affected you? Are you ready to start feeling again?

Chapter 6: God's Truth > My Truth

If we let the world dictate what we believe about God, we will get it wrong. Only God has the authority to dictate his truth. What surprised you most about hearing God's unabashed truth?

Where have you ignored God's truth and substituted your own?

How are you trying to live in your own strength?

What is God showing you about his truth?

How is he showing you that he is thinking differently than you do?

Do you think that maybe God is pruning you?

Chapter 7: An Awesome God

After God shows us how he is to be respected, he is then free to show us his amazing character. What have you learned about God's character?

What message of love is God showing you?

How might your trials glorify God?

What tools has God given you to get through your trial?

In the story of Sarah's struggles and the lesson of the cup of water and the river, what represents the cup you are asking for? What do you think is the river God wants for you?

What are some verses you can write down in a journal or on note cards to help you remember God's nature and help?

Did you discover God in a new way? How?

Write something in your life that turned out better, even though it was different from how you thought it should be.

Chapter 8: Faith Refined by the Fire and Fueled with Joy

The conclusion of a trial is renewed faith ultimately resulting in joy. What does the Jordan River, overflowing from its banks, represent in your life?

What does the Promised Land represent to you?

What stops you from taking the step?

What stories have you heard about God's goodness? Do they apply?

Where will you ask for God's healing?

Has God healed you in ways you haven't seen until now?

Chapter 9: What Now?

When God has shown himself in our lives, we have the honor and duty to share what he has done in our lives to give hope and comfort to others.

How has your faith grown because of a recent trial?

In what new ways have you experienced God?

What happened today that you knew was God's doing?

Now, write out those things in a testimony; a statement of your relationship with God.

List three other people with whom you can share this testimony of refined faith.

Now go tell them!

Notes:

Notes:

Notes: